The Danse Macabre *of Women*

Asprice iudicui hoc metuendum iudice tanto
Qui vocat et venit ista timenda dies

La mort

Je direz vous rié
nouueau
Ma dis sat theologienne
Du testament vieulx
ou nouueau
Vous soiez comme
te vous mesme
Et estes ta fort saienne
Il fait bon cecy recon
gnoistre
Et a bien mourir
mettre peine
Cest beaucoup que de
soy congnoistre

La theologienne

Femme qui de
clergie respond
pour auoir bruit ou
quon lescoute
Est dimoriies de petit pô
Qui ont grans peuly
et ne voient goutte
Sage est q rondement si
boute
Et qui trop veult sau
est beugle
Le hault monter sou
uent cher couste
Chun en sô fait a meucle

31 VERSO
Death and the Theologian
(*Poem on p. 78*)

The
DANSE MACABRE
of Women

Ms. fr. 995 of the Bibliothèque Nationale

Edited by Ann Tukey Harrison

with a chapter

by Sandra L. Hindman

The Kent State University Press

Kent, Ohio, and London, England

© 1994 by The Kent State University Press
Kent, Ohio 44242
ALL RIGHTS RESERVED
Library of Congress Catalog Card Number 93-16139
ISBN 0-87338-473-3
Manufactured in the United States of America

Library of Congress Cataloging-in-Publication Data
Danse macabre des femmes. English & French (Old French).
   The danse macabre of women : ms. fr. 995 of the Bibliothèque
nationale / edited by Ann Tukey Harrison ; with a chapter by Sandra
L. Hindman.
      p.   cm.
   Includes bibliographical references and index.
   ISBN 0-87338-473-3
   1. Dialogues, French—Translations into English. 2. Women—
Poetry. 3. Death—Poetry. I. Harrison, Ann Tukey, 1938–
II. Hindman, Sandra, 1944–   . III. Bibliothèque nationale
(France). Manuscript. Français 995. IV. Title.
   PQ1561.D3613   1994
   841'.2—dc20   93-16139

British Library Cataloging-in-Publication data are available.

For My Mother

Contents

Preface

THE *Danse Macabre des Femmes* presented here is a fifteenth-century French poem found in a lavishly illuminated late medieval manuscript (Bibliothèque Nationale fonds français 995). It describes thirty-six women, one after the other, called suddenly in the midst of their bustling daily lives to join the eternal Dance of Death. Young and old, rich and poor, widow, matron, and child, each is the focus of two short poems written in the form of a dialogue (Death calls and the victim replies) and accompanied by a miniature painting. The verses and illustrations offer a fleeting commentary on the women's lives or work, what people, possessions, or activities have meaning for them, and sometimes a hint of whether their future may hold salvation or damnation. The colorful procession of many different types of women is preceded by speeches from the four Musicians of Death and a moralizing male figure identified as *Acteur* (author/authority), all of whom urge readers of the manuscript to consider the conditions of their souls and the priorities of their lives.

The combined text and illumination form a social document with potentially valuable information about the three dozen French women who step from the homes and streets of Paris at the turn of the sixteenth century and share their preoccupations, their pleasures, and their attitudes toward death and the life they are leaving. The manuscript thus affords an occasion for social, historical, and anthropological insight. Because it postdates the popular printed editions published by Guyot Marchant in Paris beginning in 1486, it also offers an opportunity to study the dynamic interactions between manuscript and print, between popular and high culture, in the early years of the Renaissance.

Chapter 1 focuses on the poem, its origin, a stemma of its surviving versions, its authorship, its theme, its treatment of women, and its place in the danse macabre as a genre. The

ix

many illuminations of B.N.fr. 995, one full-figure portrait per folio, derive from the verses that accompany them. They also inform any reading by offering a complementary or supplementary set of attitudes through images. Chapter 2, contributed by art historian Sandra Hindman, focuses on the changes in content in the illuminations of B.N.fr. 995 and the hand-colored woodcuts in a printed incunable that preceded the manuscript. Hindman concentrates on the "upgrading" of the imagery in the manuscript, which she attributes to its execution in an aristocratic milieu of the court.

Following these two chapters, photographic reproductions of manuscript folios face a transcription of the folio text and an English translation. In the English version, every attempt has been made to retain the syntax of the original, in which the normal unit is the line. The English follows the original as closely as possible in both text and illustration in order to lead the reader back to the folio. Because the scribe's hand is generally clear, the letters both large and fairly well formed, and because the poem's language is often straightforward, it is hoped that the original sentences and phrases will be accessible to readers from many disciplines and backgrounds, even to those with rather rudimentary French skills. Three appendixes supplement the work: Appendix A, the variorum, is a list of the content variants among the seven extant manuscripts. Appendix B contains a formal description of the manuscript and its provenance, while Appendix C offers catalogue descriptions of other manuscripts and printed editions.

Illuminated manuscripts were originally interdisciplinary efforts, and this edition seeks to replicate that concept by drawing on the expertise of several scholars to provide analysis and interpretation. I wish to thank Sandra Hindman for her contribution as well as Robert Mareck for his translation of the Latin lines found in this manuscript. I am further grateful to the American Council of Learned Societies for a travel grant. Finally, I wish to acknowledge the support of my mother, Dr. Ruth S. Tukey-Bates, whose generous gift made possible the color plates in this volume. It is my hope that because of the insight it provides, this *Danse Macabre des Femmes* may ultimately be remembered as a Women's Dance of Life.

The Text

THE MANUSCRIPTS
AND THE PRINTED EDITIONS

THE EXISTENCE of the *Danse Macabre des Femmes* has been known for well over a century, and the work survives in five manuscripts and two printed editions:

A. Bibliothèque Nationale fonds français 1186, dated 1482.
B. Nouvelles Acquisitions françaises 10032, no year available.
C. Bibliothèque Nationale fonds français 25434, no year available.
D. First printed edition, from Guyot Marchant, dated 1486.
E. Second printed edition, from Guyot Marchant, dated 1491.
F. Bibliothèque Nationale fonds français 995, no year available.
G. Arsenal 3637, dated 1519.

The first modern edition of the poem was published in 1869. The editor, P.-L. Miot-Frochot, like many scholars of his day, did not adhere to the rigorous conventions of manuscript transcription normally followed today. He combined lines from several manuscripts without explanation, illustrated his edition with nineteenth-century adaptations of the illuminations in F redesigned to imitate woodcuts, and modified lines of text without comment. Although his volume is attractive and readable, it is not reliable by modern standards. Louise Götz published a meticulous transcription of C, one of the manuscripts Miot-Frochot used, in 1934. Because this is the cleanest of the five surviving manuscripts, her version of the poem can be called definitive. For Pierre Champion, it was the printed text that seemed most appropriate for reproduction, and in 1925, he published a facsimile of D.[1] The interest of Champion and his readers was primarily in the poem, and like many didactic pieces of its time, the *Danse Macabre des Femmes* cannot stand as remarkable literature. It is rather the unique combination of text with illuminations that makes an arresting social and historical document.

The development of the text, through this series of manuscripts and printed versions, is basically one of expansion: from thirty to thirty-six roles; from a stark enumeration offered without commentary to an elaborately framed tableau, decorated and made emphatically and explicitly didactic; from a monolingual poem to a composition that purports to enhance the reader's knowledge of French and Latin. The construction of a stemma is facilitated by the relatively large number of progressive alterations.

The thirty figures of A constitute the minimal corpus of the poem. All other versions contain more roles. The manuscript's date (1482, the earliest on record), the number of women depicted, and the particular placement of one woman, the *Vieille Damoiselle*, serve to separate A from all other manuscripts and printed editions. B and C contain two additional women, *la Vieille* and *la Sorciere*, and D (the 1486 printing) shows two more: *l'Abesse* and *la Prieure*. The order of the roles is further altered in F in that eight roles are put in a different order, a radical departure from A, B, and C. The accretion of roles and their placement suggest that it may be possible to assign B and C to an intermediary chronological position in the early 1480s, after A and before D. Two roles that appear first in E (the second printed edition, dated 1491), *la Bigote* and *la Sotte*, are also found in manuscript F, where they are the last women in the dance. The version of F is the longest and most complete because it contains the greatest number of roles (thirty-six). Finally, G (1519), a truncated manuscript missing the opening Queen, has only twenty-eight figures. Their order corresponds exactly with A, even to the position of the Vieille Damoiselle. There are some editorial changes in role names, and one woman is dropped from the dance altogether, but it is possible to conclude a direct connection between A and G because of the number of roles, their order, and, in particular, the location of the Old Spinster.

As the roles proliferated, the textual framework surrounding the original poem expanded. Initially in A it consisted of a brief two-stanza epilogue, spoken by *Acteur* and *la Mort* respectively, and a single Patroness stanza in which the reader is exhorted to pray "Pour celle qui cy la fait faire" (For her, the one who is having this made). B contains the same two-stanza epilogue but is accompanied by different headings (*la*

Mort and *les Morts*, not *Acteur* and *la Mort*). Also, only the first word of the Patroness stanza appears. In C, a prologue spoken by Acteur has been added; Acteur also speaks the epilogue, an arrangement that assures a certain formal balance. The Patroness stanza is completely suppressed and does not appear in D, E, or F. As one would expect, it is present in G.

It is in the printed editions that the architecture of the *Danse Macabre des Femmes* becomes fully articulated. The poem is here preceded by a page containing a message from the printer, a page featuring Acteur, and a page presenting the four skeletal musicians of death. The poem is followed by a second Acteur speaking to the Dead Queen for several folios. The initial Acteur and musician pages are complicated both in their messages and in the composition of individual elements. The Acteur folio has, in fact, four components: a Latin poem across the top of the page; a large woodcut showing Acteur seated in his study; a cartoon balloon speech in Latin issuing from Acteur; and a text in French, from Acteur to the readers. Only the very last, fourth element, the written prologue, is found partially or wholly in manuscripts prior to 1486. While Acteur in print introduces the central theme of the poem, the call to repentance, the printer on the preceding page advertises the linguistic and pedagogic merits of the edition:

> Ce present livre est appelie Miroer salutaire pour toutes gens: et de tous estaz, et est de grant utilite: et recreatio, pour pleuseurs ensengnemens tan en latin comme en francoys lesquelx il contient. Ainsi compose pour ceulx qui desirent acquerir leur salut: et qui le voudront avoir.

> This present book is called a Mirror beneficial for all people: both from all classes and it is of great utility: and renewal, for the many wise instructions in Latin as well as in French which it contains. Thus, composed for those who wish to gain their salvation and who will wish to keep it.

In F, both the separate Acteur prologue folio and the musicians' folios are retained as an introduction to the poem proper. The second Acteur epilogue folio, a dialogue with the Dead Queen, and the verses directed to the readers end the poem definitively. The concluding sections are also found in D and E but in slightly different arrangements. E also includes additional pious poems that make this printed edition a work of popular devotion.

The maintenance of this structure is not the only evidence of a close relationship between the two printed editions (D and E) and the manuscript that will be studied extensively here,

B.N.fr. 995 (F). There is only one content variant, that is a difference in the meaning of lines as opposed to spelling, between F and D. In contrast, content variants between F, A, B, C, and G are abundant. In addition to this close correlation of the two French texts, there are certain Latin verses common to both F and D alone. (These Latin lines do not appear in E.) The claim, voiced by the printer in D, that the 1486 edition of the *Danse Macabre des Femmes* might serve as a pedagogical tool for the learning of Latin as well as French was made plausible by the inclusion of the Latin quatrains accompanying the poem, which are placed at the top of each page throughout the printed edition. The verses treat death and therefore reinforce the general theme of the texts printed. The person who composed F took the Latin quatrains from D, split them into couplets, and distributed them, two lines to a folio, throughout F. Since there were not enough quatrains to supply a couplet for all folios, the manuscript designer, after leaving a few folios bare, began to include Latin couplets from sources other than D. There is no recognition of any linguistically didactic function for Latin in the manuscript; although their content does relate to the greater theme of the work, the couplets appear to be primarily decorative.

Most medieval manuscripts are like modern-day anthologies: they contain many poems assembled under the direction of one person. It is always important to examine the placement of a particular poem: Where did the manuscript redactor put the text? What is its context within a given manuscript? Although its catalogue description cites only three works in A, in actuality B.N. 1186 contains several dance poems, grouped under the title *Danse aux aveugles*, between Christine de Pizan's *Epistre Othéa* and the danses macabres of Men and Women. The order of the poems included in A is *Epistre Othéa, La Danse aux aveugles, La Danse Cupidon, La Danse de Fortune, La Danse de la mort, La Danse macabre des hommes,* and *La Danse macabre des femmes*. There are 107 folios in A, and *la Danse macabre des femmes* occupies ten of them.

B is a much longer collection: 280 folios containing twenty sections, each of which is composed of one or more discrete texts. Four of the texts bear the word *miroir* (mirror) in their title, and the *Danse Macabre des Hommes* and the *Danse Macabre des Femmes* are labeled "La Dance machabrée" and "La Danse des femmes" respectively. Within the poem, the poet conceives of his work as a place in which the reader can perceive images or reflections of his or her own life. There are no other dance works but instead a preponderance of didactic religious pieces. Most are meditative, and there are three debates, including *Le Débat de l'homme et de la femme*. Although there seems to be no special emphasis on women reflected in the choice of texts, there is a four-folio *Miroir des dames et des demoiselles* and an eight-folio section, *Jardin esperituel pour religieux et religieuses*, that describes both female and male religious. The manuscript would seem to be composed for both men and women, an assemblage of works of piety. Finally, although the danses macabres of men and women are listed separately with nonanalogous titles, they do appear next to each other.

C's 137 folios also contain a generous number of poems. Here, for the first time, *des Hommes* is separated from *des Femmes*, only one of five poems to be accorded a named author. The other four are Alain Chartier, *Breviaire des Nobles*, Pierre d'Ailly, *Les Enfermetez du corps*, Christin de Pisan [*sic*], *Bons Enseignements touchant le monde*, and George Chastellain, miscellaneous lyrics. The first text in C, *Le débat de l'homme mondain et de son compaignon qui veult estre religieux*, also occurs in B, where only one work (item 12) stands between it and *des Hommes* (item 14). Here, the *Débat* opens the manuscript, and the men's dance of death immediately follows. Unlike A and B, this collection has three sections in Latin, and two of the three are grouped together. The danses macabres of men and women are the only dances; there are no miroirs, and the common theme is didacticism, both moral and pietistic. The biblical Ten Commandments put into French verse stand beside the *Bons Enseignemens touchant le monde* (written by Christine de Pizan for her son), near the little *Cinq choses causantes la peste, commencant par F., c'est assavoir: Faim, Fruictz, Femme, Frayeur et Front*. Women receive no special attention, and there are only two titular references to death: in the *Danse Macabre des Hommes* and the *Dit de la mort* (Account of death), texts situated next to each other.

D, E, and F show strikingly similar collections. In each case, the number of individual works included in the whole is small (three to five items), and the same poems appear. The 1486 edition contains *des Hommes*, *des Femmes*, the *Débat du corps et de l'âme*, *la Complainte de l'âme dampnée*, and *des Trois morts et des trois vifs*. F offers three of those five selections in a slightly different arrangement: *des Hommes*, *des Trois morts et des trois vifs*, and *des Femmes*.

Based upon a comparison of (1) number of roles, (2) the order of those roles, (3) the type of poetic framework accompanying each work, (4) variants, (5) the context of the poem, and (6) known dates of some manuscripts and editions, it is possible to establish the following stemma:

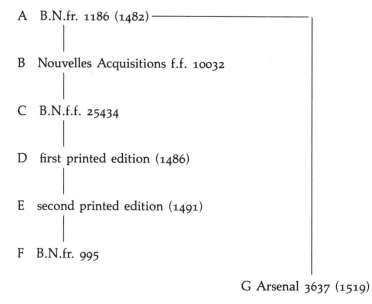

A   B.N.fr. 1186 (1482)

B   Nouvelles Acquisitions f.f. 10032

C   B.N.f.f. 25434

D   first printed edition (1486)

E   second printed edition (1491)

F   B.N.fr. 995

G Arsenal 3637 (1519)

Although G has the latest date (1519) and is thus chrono-
logically farthest from A, the texts are very close with respect
to several crucial points. Only these two manuscripts contain
the Patroness stanza, and both of these manuscripts show the
Vieille Damoiselle at a certain point in the dance. The choice
and order of roles is generally identical in these two manuscripts
with three small exceptions: G does not contain the Queen
because the manuscript is defective; it does not include the
Damoiselle role; and it reverses the roles of the Regent and the
Knight's Wife. All other manuscripts and both printed editions
differ from G and A in the number of roles and their sequence.
It therefore seems logical to conclude that G descends directly
from A without any intermediary steps and that it was revised
slightly.

The accretion of roles supports four stages of development
from 1482 to the early sixteenth century. The first stage contains
A with its thirty roles. B and C, both with thirty-two roles,
make up the second stage. The third stage, containing D and
E, has thirty-four roles, yet E is also linked with F (thirty-six
roles) to make up the fourth stage. The absence of a prologue
to introduce the roles (as in A), the presence of the first word
of the Patroness stanza, and the continuing placement of *des
Hommes* next to *des Femmes* without intervening works indicate
that B is close to A. C, with no remnant of the Patroness stanza
and separation of the danses macabres of men and women,
would therefore be dated slightly after B. The presence of both
prologue and epilogue with headings makes C resemble the 1486
printing, but the separation of *des Hommes* from *des Femmes*
in the manuscript and the number of roles differentiate C from

D. The number and order of roles, the nature of the poetic framework, the visual identity of content (that is, absence of all content variants save one), the presence of Latin couplets, and the context of other works in the same manuscript make it clear that we are dealing on the one hand with textual interaction between manuscript and print and, on the other, with a simple manuscript-to-manuscript transmission.

Although there are indications of authorship, editorship, and patronage in most of the five manuscripts and the two printings of this poem, the matter is not ascertainable. A ends with the Patroness stanza, referring to "celle qui cy la fait faire." The form and physical placement of the stanza in the manuscript, the script and spacing, seem to attach it to the poem only and not to the entire manuscript. It is possible, however, that the terminal stanza designates the greater project's benefactress of executrix. G preserves the Patroness stanza at the end of the text.

B contains the first word of the Patroness stanza ("Explicit") and describes the poem elliptically as "composée à Paris par . . ." [sic]. C attributes the women's dance of death to Martial d'Auvergne ("laquelle composa Martial d'Auvergne"), an authorship that has been accepted by Jean Rychner as well as d'Auvergne's only biographer, Vilho Puttonen. At the end of Pierre Champion's facsimile (D), recognition is given to Guyot Marchant, the printer, for both printing and composition ("composée et imprimée par Guyot Marchant"); there is no mention of d'Auvergne.[2] F credits no one, and G cites Denis Catin, again using the verb *composer*. This verb can refer to editing functions, such as deleting or adding roles, changing the names of roles, and minor alteration of lines, or it can describe invention of the poem. It is highly unlikely, if not impossible, that Denis Catin or Guyot Marchant wrote the original *Danse Macabre des Femmes*. Arguments based on external evidence can neither support nor deny d'Auvergne's authorship.[3] The fact that he is not cited in the earliest extant manuscript is certainly troublesome, and it may be that he should be considered the primary redactor or principal editor of the poem rather than its original author.

THE THEME AND ITS PUBLIC

The earliest Dance of Death of any kind is the *Danse Macabre des Hommes*, which occurred as a self-contained, discrete item in its first described appearance of record.[4] Tradition says that the prominent Parisian intellectual Jean Gerson, chancellor of the Sorbonne, composed the poem to accompany large paintings on the external walls of the Cimetière des Innocents in

1424. No copy of those verses survives, but Gerson scholars have reconstructed the genealogy of the work through a series of manuscripts and printed editions, appearing at first without the *Danse Macabre des Femmes* and then, after 1482, with it. Its initial composition, first date, authorship, and exact number of roles may be open to debate, but there is no doubt that *des Hommes* preceded that of women, for which it apparently served as a model in general form, tone, and content. From the beginning, *des Hommes* consisted of a series of sixteen-line dialogues between Death or Death's representative and the individual victims who responded to its call. Virtually all of the verses are in alternating voices of the dead and the living in sets of eight-line stanzas. The opening sentence is frequently appellative, imperative, or hortatory in its syntax, and the final line of each stanza is often an aphorism, generalization, or proverblike pronouncement. However many roles there may be, they are ordered in social hierarchy from the more powerful (Pope, Emperor) to the least powerful (Franciscan, Child). Although Death and the victims certainly lose no opportunity to fulfill a didactic function, a separate Acteur, or authority figure, appears first at the end of the women's dance and then is added to the beginning of the men's.[5] Elements present in *des Hommes* and then limited in *des Femmes* include Death speaking to and with the living, hierarchical organization, authority figure formally presenting the dance poem itself, didactic purpose and theme, and syntactic patterns within the eight-line stanzas.

The theme of the *Danse Macabre des Femmes* is the sudden, inevitable event of death, the great social leveler. By witnessing life's end, readers may be moved to evaluate their prior behavior, to repent, and, by changing their conduct, to attain salvation. The popularity of this subject in the arts of the late Middle Ages is well attested and usually attributed to a combination of the frequency of sudden, violent death in daily life and the psychological trauma resulting from the great plagues sweeping intermittently through western Europe from 1348 onward. Paris suffered epidemics in 1412, 1418, 1432–34, 1438, 1449–50, 1466–68, 1471, 1475, 1481–84 (crucial years in the life of this particular poem), and 1499–1500.[6] The theme is not new or unique to this text.

Although in other works of the period the grisly steps of corporal decomposition and putrefaction are presented in graphic detail, only rarely does this author emphasize these aspects. The skeletal musicians of death linger over images of worms eating tender flesh and heaps of bones, but neither for Acteur nor for la Mort is the physical process of decay significant.

Three women in the dance mention conventional elements usually associated in literature with dying: the Damoiselle says that her body will be given to worms and decay, the *Nouvelle Mariee* is told that she will be put into the ground, and the Sorciere hears about the cemetery. In all three references, this idea is subordinated to the stanza's content, and in two of them, the poet converts rather trite words into a poetic image. To the Damoiselle, la Mort speaks of banquets and rose cologne, a fragrance used to mask the smell of bodily decay. The whole focus of this woman's portrait is on the grooming of her person, her clothing, her beauty, which would attract the husband she seeks. Thus, to hear her use *pourriture* to describe her own body is striking, as the word choice reinforces an image that transcends the conventional. When Death tells the Newlywed that she will be put in the ground, she replies that Death weighs heavily on her. Her response provides a better context for the formulaic *serez mise en terre*, adding to these words a suggestion of sexual passivity associated with her situation in life. Except for these brief passages, the physical process of death and dying is not of interest to the poet, who uses other emphases to direct readers to a reevaluation of their lives.

From its beginning, the danse macabre of both men and women had deep Parisian roots. If the 1424 frescoes painted on the bonehouse walls of the Church of the Holy Innocents were the first visual Dance of Death ever created, Paris would be the site where this unusually popular art form made its debut. It was a Parisian printer, Guyot Marchant, who decided, sixty years after the murals, to publish the text of the *Danse Macabre des Hommes*, whose author was supposed to be Jean Gerson. A fellow Parisian, Martial d'Auvergne, is the only attributed author of the *Danse Macabre des Femmes*. Thus, this poem both originated and flourished in fifteenth-century Paris. Yet another connection is the language of this version of the poem: Parisian Middle French.

Paris is also reflected in the verses directly, in a number of references to places and events. In one section, the poet mentions the Lendit Fair, held every June in the plain of St. Denis, located to the north of the city. In another stanza he names the Petit Pont, one of the community's oldest bridges, antedating the Roman occupation. The first street directory of Paris, printed by P. le Caron in 1489, lists a rue des Recommanderesses in the Quartier des Halles, on the right bank, near the rue de la Mégisserie.[7] Neither utopian nor vaguely universal, the danse macabre of women presents recognizable people and places from an identifiable moment in a known city, and part of the verisimilitude of the women's portraits derives from their precisely localized setting.

The figure of Authority is quintessentially Parisian. Perhaps descended from preaching street friars, he wears full academic regalia, and behind him stands figuratively the power, both temporal and spiritual, of the University of Paris. Speaking *ex cathedra*, Authority is backed implicitly by two of the most influential institutions of medieval Paris: the university and the church.

Although the external form of *des Femmes*, including the identity of many in the work, was received and not invented, the choice of some roles must have fallen to the author due to the lack of symmetrical female figures. For seventeen of the thirty-one male roles in the dance, there is simply no female counterpart.[8] The poet may have been forced to invent new participants, choosing women who are either familiar Parisian types (e.g., the *Théologienne* of the Petit Pont) or who represent the kinds of workers an upper middle class Parisian household would have encountered or employed (such as the *Recommanderesse*). While the roster is not an inventory of the occupations open to women in fifteenth-century Paris, one can speak of an urban bias in the choice of roles. Mimesis increases for those figures that represent potential neighbors or servants (for example, la Vieille, a former servant, or *la Femme mignote*, as compared to *la Bergère*).

Once a role was included in the dance, it remained in subsequent texts from 1482 on, but the names of some roles, for which individualizing terms were not current or about which there was no consensus, show variation—that is, the poetic lines describing the role do not change, but the name for the role differs from one manuscript or print-setting to another. In some cases there are as many as four different names distributed through the six surviving versions. The latest manuscript has the greatest number of different role names, twelve in all, which probably results from the relative temporal and geographic separation of this text from all others: it was composed in Rheims in 1519.

Because of its didactic tone and because this work treats only women, it is potentially a primary source concerning attitudes about women in this place and time. There are only two socially negative roles included, the Witch and the Whore, and both are treated with sympathy and some degree of respect. Although several women are preoccupied with their clothing, jewelry, and social life, there is only one generalization on this topic, which is when la Mort says to the *Femme de l'escuier*, "Many a woman sins by her dress." The Femme mignote, concerned with her rings, shoes, and affluency, finally cites every woman's repentance at the moment of dying: "A woman in sin dies with regret." Interest in grooming and apparel is not overstated in this poem when compared with other writings of the period.

In the call to the Damoiselle, Death notes that "Women are the cause of many things." This may be an indictment of the traditional manipulator-temptress descended directly from Eve, or it may describe the socialite's function as organizer, an interpretation a modern reader of the text may accept more easily than a reader in the fifteenth century.

Only one other negative stereotype, the proclivity to gossip and chatter, is mentioned in the text, and the poet attaches this characteristic to the *Baillive*, for whom it is the principal identification. In the summons, la Mort notes her many critical comments about others in conversation at church, and the Baillive defends her actions by attributing them to women in general, muting even this negativity with the final assertion, "There's nothing perfect in the world." On the whole, the *des Femmes* is objective in its presentation of women, and it certainly is not misogynistic. The faults attributed to participants in this danse macabre arise from their situations in life and its temptations, not from a nature basically flawed from the beginning. The portraits, though similar in outline and theme, are individualizing and offer a variety of traits, both bad and good. Each woman is representative, but none of them is a caricature or stereotype.

Historians Suzanne Wemple and Diane Kaiser find clues in the text as to the salvation or damnation that awaits each woman called. They assert that "seventeen admit to being sirens while only thirteen accept their coming fates with reliance in God's judgment." They make a correlation between social class and salvation, finding therein sympathy for the lower classes on the part of the author, and their rather severe conclusion is that "these women, with few exceptions, should have been more aware of the eventuality of the judgment of their souls."[9] For them, the disregard of the afterlife in favor of the present is evidence of Huizingian materialism. As indicated by the title of their essay, "Death's Dance of Women," the figures depicted in the text are puppets, and while the poem and late medieval mentality may permit such an interpretation, there are interpretations more vital and positive, which this text may also allow.

Because of its purpose, this work is a valid model for the examination of late medieval didacticism in practice. Author and illuminator have used a variety of techniques to enhance the teaching impact of the work. For example, the dialogue form of summons and response carries the immediacy of direct address in every speech by la Mort. Death's words ostensibly to the victim are also spoken to the reader, and the participants in the dance expect to be overheard. The poet can rely on two levels of audience reception: the hearers within the text and the hearers of the text.

Like a play, *des Femmes* contains characters speaking lines to one another and moments when the figures turn to the audience to preach directly. Late in the dance, la Mort calls to the readers without any fictional intermediary. She describes her victim, la Sorciere, in the third person, thereby both bypassing the Witch and objectifying her. La Mort opens with the formulaic "Oyez, Oyez," and readers are instantly turned into The Public, their witness function made formal. The Witch, in her response, maintains the fiction of a trial, offers her own defense, and begs readers directly for deeds of piety on her behalf. By this manipulation of the dialogue form, readers are led to a social stance more neutral than sympathetic. Communal values have supplanted individual ones, and the medium has subtly altered the message.

Proverbs and aphorisms are frequently placed in the last line of each stanza. The persuasive force of the text is strengthened through alliance with the assumptions and assertions of the popular wisdom, and this resonance with folk authority is situated in a position of strategic value as the final words heard, the culmination, the ultimate argument. The reader is thereby convinced to accept the whole passage because the final point was an idea familiar and believed.

The framework gradually added to the dance poem further exteriorizes the instructional purpose of the work. Unlike the presentation of roles in dialogue—the Musicians of Death, Acteur, the Dead Queen—the closing ballads are aimed at the reader. Their message is presented in these passages in its simplest form. The iconography of the Acteur figure, including his clothing and surroundings, emphasizes the importance of his words. He is easily recognized as the representative of university and church, sitting in his study or standing in the cemetery at graveside.

Two final aspects found only in B.N.fr. 995 represent vestigial contributions to the didacticism of *des Femmes*: the occasional Latin couplets and the iconography of the borders. Marchant called attention to the pedagogical value of the Latin interspersions and asserted that this work of art was, therefore, a vehicle for language-learning. The designer of B.N.fr. 995 included Latin verses without comment. As for the symbolic meaning of the flowers and creatures in the borders, there is no consistent pattern of use.

Whoever the poet was, the decision to create a danse macabre peopled wholly by women is an act intriguing to us, five hundred years after the fact, in our age of heightened consciousness about women and their historical, anthropological, economic, and artistic roles. I believe that neither increased female reader-ship, nor the guiding will of a patroness, nor interest in social verisimilitude are sufficient bases for this choice of subject in and of themselves, although one or all of them may have been influential factors. The manuscripts' contexts provide evidence of a tacit recognition of works by and about women as an interesting organizing principle in manuscript composition. I believe that the single most crucial element in the choice may have been an aesthetic consideration: the desire to create a balanced set of matched figures, thirty-one men, thirty-one women. Rather than merely expanding the list of male partic-ipants to include more roles, the poet developed the concept of the pair to its logical conclusion, two paired poems. If the wish to design two symmetrical dances was not the telling impulse in the poem's inception, it surely was of paramount importance in the design of B.N.fr. 995, which is a tryptych: *Danse Macabre des Hommes, des Trois morts et des trois vifs, Danse Macabre des Femmes.*

Thus, B.N.fr. 995 is not merely one of a series of presen-tations of this text. It is the culmination of several decades and editions of the work, growing from an unadorned minimal poem probably composed in the early years of the 1480s to a carefully decorated and framed work of art, fully embellished in a formal textual setting, with potential that even its original author may never have suspected.

NOTES

1. P.-L. Miot-Frochot, ed., *La Grant Dance Macabre des Femmes que composa Maistre Marcial de Paris*; Louise Götz, "Martial d'Auvergne," 318–34; Pierre Champion, ed., *La Danse Macabre de Guy Marchant.*

2. Jean Rychner, ed., *Les Arrêts d'Amour de Martial d'Auvergne,* xxii; Vilho Puttonen, *Etudes sur Martial d'Auvergne,* 53–55. Because his edition of the poem is based upon the 1486 incunable, Champion emphasizes the role of the printer responsible for that publication. Nowhere does Champion address the question of original authorship, and his skepticism of the matter may be read as skepticism of the traditionally accepted attribution to Martial d'Auvergne.

3. Martial d'Auvergne composed three major works: *Les Arrêts d'Amour* (circa 1460), *Les Vigiles de la Mort de Charles VII* (1477–84), and *Les Dévotes Louanges à la Vierge Marie* (early 1480s). His claim to authorship of *La Danse Macabre des Femmes* is strengthened by resonance with the style and themes of these three works.

The *Arrêts* is a collection of fifty-one fictional appeal cases, dealing with the relationships between sweethearts. The language is that of the legal brief, and its stilted formalisms contrast with the trivial, whimsical, extravagant conduct of the lovers whose affections and problems are exposed in mock hearings held in the Court of Appeals of Judge Love. The work was widely circulated and imitated, and it survives in over fifty editions. In the women's dance of death, the language of two roles (the *Baillive* and the *Sorciere*) is peppered with legalisms, but the tone of the work is also light and reminiscent of the *Arrêts* in other passages.

Les Vigiles de la mort de Charles VII show the poet as chronicler, relating the events of the reign of King Charles VII within the form of the *Officium defunctorum*. Throughout the fifteen thousand lines, the author never ceases to beat the insistent cadence of moral edification, which also dominates the *Danse Macabre des Femmes*.

Martial's final effort, *Les Dévotes Louanges à la Vierge*, only six thousand lines long, relates the life and miracles of Mary, with lessons interspersed recounting Martial's own religious feelings, his faith in Mary, and comments on prevalent social ills. He is particularly engaging when describing the pitiful plight of women as he does in the Seventh Lesson, which contains passages of sympathetic realism similar to the depiction of poor women or social outcasts in the *Danse Macabre des Femmes*.

It may be that because these three works by Martial d'Auvergne manifest legalism, didacticism, piety, and sympathy for women that the attribution to him of the dance of death of women has usually seemed plausible.

4. J. Saugnieux, *Les Danses macabres de France et d'Espagne*, 32, 115.

5. Early scholars identified *Acteur* as Dr. Macabre, and they concluded that he had written the poem that seemed to bear his name. For a discussion of this false author identification see Champion, *La Danse Macabre*, 2–3. I find the note by Edelgard Dubruck on the origins of *macabre* to be the most informative treatment of a vexing, unsolved problem. See "Another look at 'macabre'," 536–43.

6. See T. S. R. Boase, *Death in the Middle Ages*; Pierre Chaunu, *La Mort à Paris*, 183–84.

7. Robert Laffont et al., ed., *Illustrated History of Paris*, 67, illustration no. 171.

8. Pope, cardinal, patriarch, constable, astrologer, canon, carthusian, sergeant, usurer, doctor, lover, lawyer, minstrel, curate, laborer, clerk, hermit.

9. Suzanne F. Wemple and Denise A. Kaiser, "Death's Dance of Women," 341.

The Illustrations

BY SANDRA L. HINDMAN

THE ILLUSTRATIONS of the *Danse Macabre des Femmes* are little known. Of the five extant manuscripts of the text, only F is illustrated, but it has not been studied since it was published in a partial black-and-white facsimile by Miot-Frochot in the mid–nineteenth century. Some confusion exists in the literature concerning the relationship between F and an earlier illustrated manuscript version that is alleged to be lost.[1] The two editions of the text printed by Guyot Marchant, D and E, also include illustrations that have been published in facsimile, but neither of these has been carefully examined. Without further comment, scholars simply acknowledge that manuscript F copies inaccurately the printed versions D and E.[2] It is well known that the *Danse Macabre des Hommes* predates the *Danse Macabre des Femmes*. Existing in many fresco versions from the end of the fourteenth century through the fifteenth century, the men's danse macabre was first printed in September 1485. Although these fresco and printed versions have been extensively published,[3] neither the text nor the illustrations of *des Hommes* have been analyzed in comparison with *des Femmes*.

TEXT AND ILLUSTRATION IN THE PRINTED MEN'S AND WOMEN'S *DANSES MACABRES*

The *Danse Macabre des Hommes* was apparently first illustrated in 1424 on the charnel walls of the Church of the Innocents in Paris, accompanied by French verses attributed to Jean Gerson.[4] Other fresco cycles painted in the fifteenth century in France, including those at Amiens, La Chaise-Dieu, and in Kermaria-en-Isquit,[5] are thought to copy the now-destroyed frescoes from the Church of the Innocents. Of these, only the frescoes at La

Chaise-Dieu include women, and not all include the French verses.

The first published edition of *des Hommes*, illustrated with seventeen woodcuts depicting thirty persons and accompanied by French verses presumably modeled on the images and texts painted at the Church of the Innocents, was printed by Guyot Marchant in September 1485.[6] In June 1486, he published a second edition that included six new woodcuts depicting eleven persons and accompanied by French texts, so that the total number of persons depicted increased to forty-one. One month later, Marchant published, along with a reissue of the men's dance, the first printed edition of the text of the *Danse Macabre des Femmes* (D), which he illustrated with only one new woodcut, representing Death and the Queen and Death and the Duchess.[7] In 1490, using twenty-four of Marchant's plates from the 1486 edition, Goeffroy de Marnef published a Latin translation by Pierre Desrey of the *Danse Macabre des Hommes*.[8] Then, in 1491, Marchant published a French edition of the combined men's and women's dances, E, this time with a full sequence of twenty-one woodcuts devoted to the women's dance in addition to the cuts used in the 1486 edition of the men's dance. Woodcuts of the men's and women's danses macabres in the margins of late fifteenth- and sixteenth-century French-printed Books of Hours derive from these earlier printed versions.[9] Finally, around 1500, a luxury manuscript version of the complete French text of 1491 was written and illuminated: Paris, Bibliothèque Nationale, Ms. fr. 995 (F).

Text and image in the printed *Danse Macabre des Hommes* preach the way to salvation. From the first sentence (addressed to those who "desire life eternal") to the last (for those "who do not wish to be damned"), the men's danse concerns itself with the wages of sin and the need for repentance.[10] The text warns against avarice, particularly in its characterizations of the Townsman, the Canon, the Jailer, and the Usurer. And avarice takes its place along with pride, gluttony, and intemperance as one of the seven deadly sins. At the end of the book, the Fool appears; he is a social leveler who teaches that "all dead men are equal" before God. The Dead King, appearing twice, provides a neat framing device for the work. Because of his rank, he heads the dance at the beginning of the poem, but he also concludes the sequence, following the Fool, to reiterate the power of death over people of "different conditions." Finally, Acteur urges man to "win the joy of paradise" by reflecting on the passion of Jesus Christ, the pain of hell, and the day of judgment. The many lively characterizations in the verses of *des Hommes* are overshadowed by the ominous and pervasive threat of the Last Judgment, which echoes throughout the text.

The woodcuts in the men's danse depict the confrontation between the skeletons and the living (fig. 1). The dead man usually carries an attribute, such as a sickle, a spade, or an arrow, as he approaches the living man. The living are readily identifiable by their costumes and accessories—the Pope wearing his tiara and mantle; the Emperor a garment decorated with the imperial eagle, along with his crown, an orb, and a sword. All are rendered with little expression. Some of the living, such as the Monk, the Pope, and the Bishop, raise their hands in a gesture that can be read as an attempt to forestall death.[11] But most seem prepared to accept their fates passively as they go hand-in-hand with the skeletons.

Two interrelated characteristics of the text and pictures of the printed women's danse macabre (E) set it apart from the men's: a sense of the nitty-gritty of day-to-day life and a tone of social satire. At the very beginning of the work, the four musicians of death call attention to the themes of vanity and avarice as they address all women, those "from the world and from the cloister." One musician taunts women about their vanity; another censures women for their ability to deceive themselves, cynically predicting that, rather than mending their ways, they will try to buy immortality with money.

From then on, high- and low-born women alike are described as coveting their material belongings. In the first half of the work, where the figures are mostly counterparts to those in the danse macabre of men (the King/Queen, the Duke/Duchess, the Abbot/Abbess, the Squire/Squire's Lady), the Duchess is called from her goods and jewels, the Abbess from her "cross of silver and of gold," the Squire's Lady from her muffs, caps, and fillets, and the Debutante from her brooches. In the second half, where the women represent many occupations from the lower classes, a vivid picture emerges of women operating within a mercantile and probably urban society. The Merchant Woman, for example, bids farewell to both her scale and the chair from which she watched over her employees, urging them to "sell more dearly." Now, in her absence, she fears they will only play. The Resaleswoman boasts that she earned two *ecus* in a single day by cleverly overcharging her customers. And the Old Woman, a former household servant, tells how she clothed herself with her master's money and "made hot wine from his cellar."

When in the last example the Fool, traditionally named Margot, speaks, she rounds up the "trim, pretty ladies" and calls them all to death. The name *Margot*, a diminutive of Margaret, also means magpie, the bird that chatters incessantly, or a gossip. According to the text of the poem, because Margot speaks the truth, having done nothing wrong, she asks forgiveness for the others and exonerates herself. Thus the poem ends on an ironic note with a kind of comic inversion in which the prattling female Fool is seen as less foolish than womankind in general.[12] Finally, Acteur steps in to reiterate the inevitability of death. He muses cynically that what's gone is gone, and that there is no more news about dead people, who are worth nothing to their heirs unless they have silver and plate. The entire work thus can be interpreted as culminating in a message about human nature, specifically women's inherent folly as predicated on their greed.

Using the conventions of illustrating the genre of the danse macabre as a schematic procession, the illustrator of E succeeds in conveying a sense of social satire that complements the tone of the poem. Details of costume and bearing, including pose and facial features, individualize the images. For example, the money bag dangling from the waist is a ubiquitous attribute of these figures, one that is used to signify their avarice. It is worn not only by women who represent individual occupations, like the Merchant Woman, the Hostess, the Shepherdess, the Resaleswoman, and the Wetnurse, but also by women—such as the Young Girl, the Pregnant Woman, and the Spinster—to represent different ages.[13]

In the most powerful illustrations, costume and bearing work together to convey different attitudes. The Prostitute, dressed in a fetching floral-patterned red robe and wearing a flower in her hair, teases the approaching skeleton by striking a flirtatious pose and offering him the flower (fig. 3). Next to her, the Resaleswoman tastelessly flaunts not one but two ornate necklaces that she presumably received from her wealthier customers, and she wears two money bags to hold her ill-gotten profits. The individual in the woodcut seems to be a caricature of the shrewd Merchant with her sharp, pointed features and thin, wizened body.[14] The Wetnurse, slovenly dressed in a tight-fitting bodice that reveals her bulging bosom and a scarf that does not quite cover her stringy yellow hair, brandishes a baby's rattle in one hand as she puts her other hand on her hips, scowling at the viewer and ignoring the skeleton (fig. 4). The Hosteler, who works at the outskirts of the city to find rooms for wayfarers, stoops to consult her sheet of listings for the skeleton that approaches her (fig. 5). These lifelike vignettes provoke laughter at the way women go about their daily pursuits, even at the moment of their deaths. They certainly do not inspire meditation on the day of judgment.

The transformation of the work probably reflects the change in focus from men to women. By concentrating on women, the revised dance focuses on the gender that from the perspective of popular culture was frequently mocked, considered along

with the peasant to epitomize folly, and even sometimes re-
garded as inherently evil. This attitude toward women was
reflected in innumerable proverbial sayings and folk customs
of the time, and it is no accident that the verses of the *Danse
Macabre des Femmes* make use of many proverbs and that the
poem concludes first with the corrupt, even sinister figures of
a Witch and a Hypocrite and then Margot the Fool. Thus, the
1491 edition of the women's danse macabre reveals an exploi-
tation of women for the purpose of satire.

RELATIONSHIP BETWEEN THE ILLUMINATED MANUSCRIPT AND THE PRINTED VERSIONS

Before examining the ways in which the illuminated manuscript
differs from the printed edition, it is useful to confirm that the
manuscript is based on the printed model. The process of ad-
aptation can easily be seen by comparing the folios portraying
Authority in the manuscript with a hand-colored, printed copy.
In each picture Authority is similarly posed, seated before his
desk in front of a podium or pulpit (fig. 6 and fol. 24). In the
printed book he is in the act of writing, holding down the page
of the book with his left hand and moving his pen with his
right. In the manuscript his hands are in the same position, but
as they are without the writing implement and the book, the
gestures no longer make sense. Other comparable details include
the drapery and position of his legs, the open pulpit with its display of books, the brocade backdrop, and the use of an arcade
frame. Even the colors are similar: in each picture the throne is
red, Authority's mantle is blue, and his robe is a reddish purple.
Similarities between other illustrations confirm the relationship
between the two exemplars: compare, for example, the Old
Woman (fols. 36 verso and Bi verso), the Crippled Woman (fols.
35 verso and Bii), many of the skeletons, and the Horseman of
the Apocalypse (fols. 23 and Bv verso). It would seem, therefore, that the illuminator had before him the woodcuts of the
printed book, perhaps even a hand-colored book, from which he
modeled more luxurious illuminations. Instances of manuscripts
that copy printed books are not uncommon during the first century of printing, when the handmade manuscript and not its me-
chanically reproduced counterpart remained the more familiar
form of the book.[15]

Rather than slavishly copying his model, the illuminator
freely adapted, sometimes completely transforming, the woodcuts. Among the most radical changes are the costumes and
accessories of the women. Most women in the manuscript wear
the upper-class costume that was much in vogue at the end of

the fifteenth century: a long robe, fitted at the waist, with a full skirt, wide, lined sleeves called *létices,* and a square collar; a ropelike belt called a *cordeliere;* a black hat called a *chapperon;* and flat black shoes called *soulliers.*[16] Often the robes worn by women in the miniatures are made of rich, brocaded cloth, probably satin, as in the case of the Queen, the Duchess, and the Debutante. They are also frequently lined with fur: white fur or ermine for the Queen, the Duchess, the Merchant Woman, and the Debutante, and brown fur (squirrel?) for the Squire's Wife, the Bourgeoise, the Virgin, the Hostess, and the Hosteler. Nearly every woman wears a robe that is lined if not with fur, then with cloth: the Lady Regent, the Knight's Wife, the Theologian, the Newlywed, the Pregnant Woman, the Crippled Woman, the Resaleswoman, the Young Girl, the Bride, and the Darling Wife. To go with their fancy dresses, most of the women wear an upper-class hat that is close-fitting and rounded at the forehead, and loose and straight from the crown to the neck. A few women wear an intermediate version of this hat, a *coquille,* that has a square visor at the forehead, as appears for example on the Bourgeoise, the Bailiff's Wife, the Theologian, the Newlywed, and the Hostess. Among the women in the miniatures, it is noteworthy that only five—the Wetnurse, the Shepherdess, the Village Woman, the Bathhouse Attendant, and the Chambermaid—stand out as wearing middle- or lower-class costumes.

In contrast, upper-class costume is worn in the printed version only by the Queen, the Duchess, the Lady Regent, the Squire's Wife, the Debutante, and the Theologian. Among these women, only the Queen wears a garment made of brocade and trimmed with fur. The garments of the Lady Regent, the Duchess, the Squire's Wife, the Debutante, and the Theologian are, however, wide-sleeved and lined. In place of the black chapperon, most of the middle-class women wear a red (or sometimes purple) coquille. None wears soft black soulliers; instead they wear sturdy, thick-soled, leather shoes.

A clear distinction between the dress of different classes, in line with the costumes included in the miniatures and the woodcuts, was made in the law and literature of the period. A sumptuary law passed in 1485 during the reign of King Charles VIII—the first of its kind since the end of the fourteenth century—restricted silk garments woven with gold and silver threads to the highest nobility.[17] Individuals who broke this law risked a stiff fine and the confiscation of their clothes. Nobility of the rank of *chevalier,* which was apparently determined by income, were permitted to wear all other sorts of silk garments, whereas nobility of the rank of *écuyer* could wear damask, and plain and patterned satin. Even if these sumptuary laws were largely ignored, as has been suggested, they nonetheless indicate that class differences were understood partly in terms of dress. In a poem written after 1488 and probably before 1492 on the subject of women's clothing, *Le Triumphe* or *Parement des dammes*, Olivier de la Marche also makes class distinctions.[18] For example, he specifies that women of the bourgeoisie wear red hats, black being reserved for the nobility. The illuminator clearly did not follow the guidelines dictated by social custom when he painted individuals of different classes dressed uniformly.

It could be argued that the near-exclusive use of upper-class dress in the manuscript is simply due to an illuminator who, because he was accustomed to working for the nobility, paid little attention to differences in costume and instead dressed everyone, or nearly everyone, alike in the high fashion of the day. Yet, the fact that the illuminator recorded very accurately certain other details of dress suggests that there is in the manuscript a self-consciousness with regard to costume. For example, the Old Woman wears old-fashioned, well-to-do clothing she must have bought in her youth. Her narrow-sleeved robe is belted at the waist with a wide band, a *bandier*, instead of with an up-to-date cordeliere. The collar of her dress is round rather than square, and she wears a conical hat called a *hennin*. These details date her clothing before the end of the third quarter of the fifteenth century.

Details of accessories, such as the money bags, are also changed in the manuscript. Underscoring the theme of avarice in the woodcuts, the bulging little purses appear on far fewer figures in the manuscript. Only women whose occupations directly involve them in commercial dealings, such as the Merchant Woman, the Resaleswoman, and the Hosteler, still sport money bags. Others who have no practical need for carrying such a bag do not. Thus, the Young Girl, the Pregnant Woman, and the Spinster are depicted without the money bag, as are the Lady Regent, the Chambermaid, and the Witch. The effect of this change is that the pictures in the manuscript lessen the force of the charge of avarice by suggesting that one of its customary symbols is merely a realistic accessory that befits persons who follow certain trades.

Some of the imagery in the miniatures was made richer by adding costume details not found in the 1491 illustrations. This happens in the case of a few of the religious figures, such as the Abbess and the Prioress, each of whom holds a book as an attribute, whereas in the woodcuts the Abbess holds only a staff and the Prioress holds nothing at all. The Village Woman, who carried a single basket in the woodcut, is depicted with two baskets, one filled with chickens and balanced on the top of her head, and the other, empty, held at her side, to illustrate Death's warning to her: "You won't sell eggs or cheese anymore. Go empty your basket." The Chambermaid, portrayed in the woodcut holding her keys and with the money bag dangling from her waist,[19] also holds a distaff in the illumination. The addition of the distaff not only suggests that one of the Chambermaid's household duties may have been to spin fibers to make thread or yarn, but also it serves to call attention to the verses in the poem that refer to her predilection for gossip, since the distaff was a proverbial figure for women's gossip.[20] These examples, showing the illuminator's close attention to the poem, contribute additional evidence in support of the hypothesis that the instances where the illuminations vary from the text are deliberate rather than inadvertent.

One aspect of the miniatures, the setting, offered the artist considerable opportunity for invention. Among the indoor settings, a bedroom is used for the Newlywed as well as the Darling Wife, who is "kept in the lap of luxury" and sleeps until noon. Another of the indoor settings is probably meant to be a church. A brocade cloth of honor, like that which serves as a backdrop in representations of the Virgin and Child, appears behind the Abbess, the Prioress, and the Franciscan Nun. A courtyard that provides a glimpse into a background landscape dotted with castles in the distance is the setting for some figures, such as the Debutante and the Pregnant Woman. Less frequently, landscape settings are used, as for the Shepherdess who walks with her dog jumping about her ankles in the open, hilly countryside in which appears a solitary half-timber house. With the exception of the illumination portraying the Shepherdess, the architecture is richly appointed: the floors are composed of red and green marble tiles, the walls are faced with marble of different tones, and the courtyards are constructed as grand loggias with Italianate pilasters and moldings. The courtly settings as much as the genteel costumes convey the impression that these scenes are quite remote from the urban marketplace.

Two images, those of the Witch and the Fool, are transformed in particularly interesting ways in the manuscript. Whereas the Witch in the 1491 woodcut wears a money bag and a trinket at her waist and doffs a pointed hat, the Sorceress in the miniature faces the viewer and holds her attribute, the broom, upright while she stands barefoot before a fireplace, her hair hanging loosely around her darkened face (compare fig. 7 and fol. 39 verso). The portrayal in the illumination has more in common with late medieval traditions depicting witchcraft.[21] In the 1491 woodcut the Fool is dressed in an ordinary frock, has a chicken on her cap, and carries a fool's staff (compare fig. 8 and fol. 42 verso). The presence of the chicken, a stupid bird that cackles ceaselessly, is related to the idea of the fool who talks nonsense all the time, and is characteristic of the text's portrait of Margot. In the miniature, she is elaborately costumed: she is outfitted in a male jester's suit of green and yellow, wears a pointed cap topped with an ass's ears and bells, and carries a fool's bauble on which a woman's face has been intricately carved and gilded. The image of the fool in the manuscript has more in common with the tradition of illustrating folly[22] and, perhaps more importantly, is less likely to be read as applicable to any woman because the distinctive jester's costume has replaced the commonplace garb. In the absence of such complex iconography for most of the other women in the manuscript, these images call attention to themselves. Why are they so distinctive?

Throughout the manuscript, the miniatures are upgraded. Whereas the caricatures of women in the woodcuts of the 1491 edition reinforce a satirical reading of the poem, the manuscript illuminations are more highbrow. The illuminator made little attempt to reinforce the poem's presentation of a cross-section of classes. Rather, he elevated some figures, such as the Prostitute, above their class. He also ignored the mocking tone found in his woodcut models. It is clear that the women of the manuscript illuminations inhabit a different milieu, the refined, cultivated environment of the court, where intellectual resources provide the new iconography for the Witch and the Fool. The question remains, however, whether, in upgrading the imagery, the illuminator is pro- or anti-women. To put it another way, is he emphasizing the importance and grandeur of women by dressing them uniformly as upper-class individuals, or could he be chiding them for their interest in luxury and fine clothes? A partial answer to this question comes from an examination of the differing conclusions—textual and pictorial—of the two books.

Two changes occur in the composition and sequence of text and image at the end of the manuscript. First, the sections that treat four women—the Bride, the Darling Wife, the Chambermaid, and the Hosteler—are interpolated toward the end of the manuscript between the Witch and the Hypocrite, whereas they occur much earlier in the printed editions. Although there seems to be no thoroughly satisfactory explanation for this change, it does prompt a slightly different reading of the manuscript. By separating the Witch from the Hypocrite and the Fool, the dance does not end with a series of essentially negative perspectives on women. Second, the works conclude differently. At the end of the manuscript comes Authority's epilogue on the inevitability of death written in the form of a six-stanza exhortation. A dialogue between the Dead Queen and Authority, which reuses the text of the exhortation, follows the epilogue. What is important is that, just as in the men's danse macabre, the image of the Queen at the beginning and end neatly frames the work. A miniature of a seated figure of Authority introduces the epilogue, and a miniature of Authority standing in a grave-yard next to the Dead Queen's corpse and crown introduces the concluding dialogue. In contrast, in the 1491 edition, the importance accorded the Queen is changed. The dialogue between the Dead Queen and Authority comes immediately after the sections on the Hypocrite and the Fool; instead of ending at this point, the text continues in the printed edition with another long dialogue between Death and womankind in which Death stresses the inevitability of his final coming and the women pray for forgiveness of their sins. In the 1491 edition, the first dialogue is illustrated with a woodcut of Authority and the Dead Queen, as in the manuscript. The second dialogue is illustrated with four woodcuts not present in the manuscript. The first large woodcut depicts Death on horseback before a hellmouth. Three smaller cuts placed in the margins of this section depict three women dressed in quite ordinary costumes.[23]

The different conclusions of the manuscript and the printed edition are thus in line with the different focuses of the two books. On the one hand, in the manuscript the place accorded the Queen at the conclusion of the work fits well with its emphasis on upper-class women. It reinforces a wholly positive reading of a group of elegantly dressed women, a reading that is not altogether consistent with the text. On the other hand, in the printed book the subordination of the Queen in place of women from the middle and lower classes fits with its emphasis on the commonplace and ordinary. It contributes to the spicy satire that runs throughout the book in both text and pictures. Parenthetically, the long passage added at the end of the printed work shares some features with the literature of popular devotion from which the character of the manuscript, missing this section of text, remains quite distinct.

The character of *des Femmes* connects it with a small group of didactic works of the period that focus on women's costume. A little-known antecedent to it is the *Miroir des dames*, in which Death reminds women that it effaces all beauty and brings about "the end of beautiful eyes, the end of the beauty of the face, the end of precious clothes, the end of sumptuous edifices," and so forth.[24] De la Marche's *Parement des dames* also focuses on women's dress, as the author addresses emperors, queens, princesses, ladies, girls, bourgeoisie, and servants at the beginning of the poem.[25] He then assigns each fully described item of women's clothing an allegorical meaning: shoes give diligence; from stockings come perseverance; from the garter follows a firm resolve; the purse leads to generosity; the ring signifies faith; and so forth. The sequence concludes with a list of well-

35 RECTO
Death and the Shepherdess
(Poem on p. 92)

36 RECTO
Death and the Village Woman
(Poem on p. 96)

La mort

Or oyez / on vous
fait assauoir
Tous que ceste vieille
soraeie
A fait mourir et de
cepuoir
Plusieurs gens en
mainte maniere
Est condempnee cõ
meurtriere
A mourir ne viura
plus gaire
Je la mayne en son
cymitiere
Cest belle chose de bien
faire

La soraciere

Mes bonnes gens
ayez pitie
De moy las poure pe
cheresse
Et me donnez par
amytie
Don de pastenostre ou
de messe
Jay fait du mal en
ma ieunesse
Dont icy achete sa pu
ne
Si prye dieu q̃ mon
ame adresse
Nul ne perist contre
sa fortune

39 VERSO
Death and the Witch
(Poem on p. 110)

Proth quicūqᷓ dies sibi longos estimat euui
Nulli est tota dies vnteir tuta dies

La mort

Pour vo⁹ mostrer
voſtre folie
Et quon doit sur la mort
veiller
Si la main espousee iolie
Allons nous en deshabiller
Pour vous ne fault
plus teauaillier
Car vous viendres con
cher ailleurs
On ne se dit trop res
ueiller Les faitz de
dieu sont merueilleux

Lespousee

En la tournee
equanoxe desir
Dauoir quelque ioye
en ma vie
Se nay q̃ duail z desplaisir
Et si fault q̃ tātost ſeuie
De mort pourquoy
as tu enuie
De moy qui me prens
si acoup
Si grant faulte nay
desserue
Mais il fault louer
dieu de tout

40 RECTO

Death and the Bride

(Poem on p. 112)

dressed noble ladies seized by Death. As in *des Femmes*, female finery is inserted in a *memento mori* context. Nevertheless, the reader is not meant to take too seriously the morbid message but rather, as Olivier de la Marche urges, "to enjoy the possessions that you find beautiful . . . in order to triumph and be well outfitted."

SOCIO-HISTORICAL CONTEXT
OF THE MANUSCRIPT VERSION

Although the original owner of *des Femmes* is unknown, the artist who painted the miniatures worked mostly for royal and aristocratic patrons at the French court. Ms. fr. 995 belongs with a group of manuscripts attributed to an illuminator known as the Master of Philippe of Guelders. The name comes from a painted frontispiece of the Duchess Philippe (or Philippine) of Guelders, the wife of Rene II, Duke of Lorraine and King of Naples and Jerusalem, in a specially made copy of the *Vita Christi*.[26] The Master of Philippe of Guelders worked also for King Louis XII (reigned 1498–1515), for whom he executed some miniatures in a Paris-made copy of Xenephon's *Cyropaedia*. The career of this illuminator lasted from about 1495 to 1510, dates that are consistent with the time of execution of our manuscript.[27] Based on the details of the artist's career, coupled with the deluxe character of Ms. fr. 995, there is every likelihood that our manuscript was made in Paris for an individual at the court.

Specific comparisons with manuscripts in this group help to affirm that the production of our manuscript took place in Paris for someone in the royal circle. Both the miniatures and borders in one manuscript, a Missal that belonged to the Abbey of Saint-Victoire in Paris, share characteristics with the Paris copy of the danse macabre (fig. 10).[28] The fact that this Missal belonged to St.-Victoire, even if it may not have been made for the Abbey, provides a link with Paris, as does the collaboration of the Master of Philippe of Guelders and the Master of Morgan 219, who is thought to have worked in Paris.[29] Among the manuscripts ascribed to the Master of Philippe of Guelders, Louis XII's copy of the *Cyropaedia* is one of the closest to the Paris danse macabre. Not only are certain features of the drawing, especially the faces of the women, similar, but one style of acanthus border frequently shows up in both books (compare fols. with fig. 9).[30] Another manuscript, a Viennese copy of Michel Ritz's *Changement de Fortune en toute prosperité*, is not only related to the style of the Master of Morgan 219 but also is a near twin to the Paris book with respect to much of its secondary decoration.[31] At least four of the border patterns are identical in the two manuscripts, which also share models for initials and frames (fig. 11).[32] The Vienna manuscript was made for Margaret of Austria, Duchess of Savoy, between 1507 and 1509, and it is associated with a number of other books, such as the Waddesdon Manor copy of Anne of Brittany's coronation book, made for persons of the court.[33]

Two potential patrons within the court, Anne of Brittany and Margaret of Austria, deserve special mention. Both women held positions of power and authority in their day. Both were also bibliophiles who actively sponsored works about women and to whom writers consequently addressed tracts treating women in the hope of securing their patronage. Anne of Brittany (d. 1514) is an individual of considerable historical stature because of her position and patronage.[34] Having already been Queen of France as the wife of Charles VIII, she became queen again in 1499 as the second wife of Louis XII, whose marriage to his first wife Claude had been childless and, as a result, annulled. Her biographers report that she appointed a number of women to positions that had formerly been reserved for men. A number of literary works about women are addressed to her.[35] As early as 1493, an anonymous translator of Boccaccio's *De claris mulieribus*, a work recounting one hundred stories about famous (or infamous) women of antiquity, dedicated a new French translation, *Des nobles et cleres femmes*, to Anne.[36] In 1504 she requested that her confessor, Antoine Dufour, compose a new work about the lives of certain famous women.[37] Dufour's *Vies des femmes célèbres* focused on ninety-one diverse examples that included the biblical figures of Eve and Mary, ancient representatives such as Minerva and Penthesilea, and modern individuals like Griseldis and Joan of Arc. The manuscript presented to Anne was decorated with eighty-four miniatures sometimes attributed to the workshop of Jean Bourdichon. Before 1502, Octavien de Saint-Gelais, a rhetorician, dedicated a work to Anne entitled *Vingt et une épistres des dames illustrés*, a translation of Ovid's *Heroïdes*.[38] In 1506, Jean Marot, court poet and *valet de chambre* in Anne's service, wrote for her a work entitled *La Vray disant Advocate des Dames*, which constitutes an apologia for the female sex in general and an exaltation of Anne in particular.[39]

Margaret of Austria (d. 1530) could also be considered a feminist from both political and cultural perspectives.[40] The daughter of Duchess Mary of Burgundy and Emperor Maximilian I, Margaret was destined at an early age to marry Charles VIII of France, but when he instead married Anne of Brittany, she married Juan of Castille in 1497, who died after only five months of marriage. Widowed and childless, Margaret was again thought to be suitable for a king of France, Louis XII, but Louis, after the death of Charles VIII, also married Anne of Brittany. Margaret was subsequently wed to Philip of Savoy and then became the aunt of Francis I and Charles V. In 1507, three years after Philip's death, she became the acting regent of the Netherlands during the minority of Charles V and was later made regent by her father Maximilian, a position she served until her death in 1530. She also led an active cultural life: around 1507 or 1508 she commissioned *Le Changement de Fortune en toute prosperité* from Michel Ritz, the work that recounted the many vicissitudes of her political fortunes (fig. 11). In 1509 Agrippa wrote for her a Latin tract, *De nobilitate et praeccellentia foeminei*, exalting womankind in general.[41] She commissioned other works expressing sympathies for women, including Jean Lemaire's *La Couronne margaritique*, of which the only extant copy, elaborately illustrated probably by Savoyard artists, belonged to her brother, Philip the Handsome.[42] Her extensive library, the inventory of which survives, included many manuscripts by the fifteenth-century writer Christine de Pizan, most of which address the status of women.[43] And like Christine, she tried her hand at composing poetry, which she compiled into albums.[44]

In France at the end of the fifteenth and beginning of the sixteenth centuries, there was, in fact, an exceptional number of powerful, learned women whose activities and taste fostered an environment in which works for and about women flourished. Margaret of Navarre (d. 1549), the sister of King Francis I, was a bibliophile, an advocate of women's rights, and a noted author.[45] Anne of Beaujeu (d. 1522), the daughter of Louis XI and wife of Pierre II of Bourbon, constable of France, served as regent of France between 1483 and 1486 during the minority of Charles VIII. It has even been suggested that her regency inspired the inclusion of the Lady Regent in *des Femmes*.[46] In partial imitation of Saint Louis's *Enseignements*, a book of instructions to his sons, Anne wrote an *Enseignements d'Anne de France . . . à sa fille Suzanne de Bourbon* for her daughter Suzanne (d. 1521).[47] Louise of Savoy (d. 1531), Duchess of Angoulême and the mother of Francis I, served as joint regent of France along with Anne of Brittany during the minority of Francis I. She, too, was a bibliophile.[48] Claude of France (d. 1524), wife of Francis I, commissioned deluxe Books of Hours and an illuminated *Livre du Sacré*.[49] Other powerful women of the period include Catherine of Foix, Queen of Navarre (d. 1517); Jeanne de France, Duchess of Orleans (d. 1505); Charlotte of Burgundy, wife of Jean d'Albret; Françoise d'Albret, wife of Jean de Bourgogne; and, of course, Philippe of Guelders.

Like Anne of Brittany and Margaret of Austria, these aristocratic women were interested in female models that served to elevate the status of women. Their concerns mirror the emphasis on the grandeur and importance of women in the manuscript version of *des Femmes*. Although the women's danse macabre has not so far been found in an inventory of the period, it is certainly in this milieu that its original owner must be sought.

Reflections upon the patronage of the manuscript and the circumstances of its production underscore the idea that the *des Femmes* manuscript is a very different kind of work from its printed predecessors. What is initially surprising, and even anachronistic, is the existence of a lavishly illuminated, parchment copy of the danse macabre of women. The text, which is satirical and even earthy, seems out of place in the luxurious form of the Paris manuscript. Yet, the miniatures are well suited because they were modified to accommodate the refined taste of a higher, more learned class of readers. In this setting, the *Danse Macabre des Femmes* became a work that stood in praise of women.

NOTES

1. The confusion stems from Hammerstein, *Tanz und Musik*, 177–78, who cites a second manuscript in Paris, Bibliothèque Nationale (hereafter BN), ancien fonds Colbert, Nr. 1849, MS du roi, vélin Nr. 7310, which he dates c. 1483 and believes to be the source for the illuminations in Ms. fr. 995, which he dates after 1491. Hammerstein did not realize that Ms. fr. 995 and the Colbert manuscript are one and the same, the recorded shelf marks being the former shelf marks of Ms. fr. 995. Hammerstein bases his date, c. 1483, on his supposition that the inclusion of the Lady Regent refers to the regency of Anne de Beaujeu from 1483 to 1486.

2. The illustrations of the manuscript were judged to be copies of those in the printed book by Pierre Champion, ed., *La Danse macabre de Guy Marchant*, 6.

3. See, for example, the monographic study by Helmut Rosenfeld, *Der mittelalterliche Totentanz*.

4. V. Dufour, *La Dance macabre des Saints Innocents de Paris*. Attribution to Gerson is based partly on the existence of the text in two manuscript compilations of Gerson's writings in BN, MSS lat. 14904 and fr. 25550.

5. Now destroyed, the frescoes at Amiens are depicted in a painting by Simon Marmion, which is discussed in Rosenfeld, p. 150ff. On La Chaise-Dieu, see A. Jubinal, *Explication de la danse des morts de la Chaise-Dieu* (Paris: Challamel, 1862), passim, and A. Brunereau, *La Danse macabre de la Chaise-Dieu* (Caen: E. Domin, 1923). On Kermaria-en-Isquit, see F. Soleil, *La Danse macabre de Kermaria-en-Isquit* (St. Brieux: L. Prud'homme, 1882), and L. Begule, *La Chapelle de Kermaria-Nisquit et sa danse des morts* (Paris: H. Champion, 1909).

6. This edition exists in a unique copy in Grenoble, Bibliothèque municipale, Incun. 327, which has been reproduced in facsimile by Pierre Vaillant, *La Danse macabre de 1485*.

7. For the second edition of the men's dance, see BN, Rés. Ye. 88, published in facsimile by Champion. For the first French edition of the women's dance, see ibid., Ye. 189. This edition included texts and woodcuts for *Le Débat d'un corps et d'une âme* and *La Complainte de l'âme damnée*, also published in facsimile by Champion.

8. Entitled *Chorea ab eximo Macabro versibus alemanicus edita*. A unique copy exists in Washington, D.C., Library of Congress, Rosenwald Collection, Incun., 1490. D 26, Goff D-21, reproduced in facsimile by W. Ivins, *The Dance of Death printed at Paris in 1490*.

9. BN, Rés. Ye. 86, which is hand-colored and reproduced in facsimile: *La Danse macabre des femmes; (suivie de) La Danse nouvelle des hommes; (augmentée du) Dit des trois morts et des trois vifs; (du) Débat d'un corps et d'une âme; (et de la) Complainte d'une âme damnée* (Paris: Union Latine d'éditions, 1977); F. Soleil, *Les Heures gothiques*, 69–81, 120–29. First woodcuts in a Book of Hours published in 1498 by Simon Vostre.

10. A chronology of the French editions is found in Saugnieux, *Les Danses macabres de France et d'Espagne*, 123–31.

11. See Ivins, *Dance of Death*, fols. Aiii, Aiiii verso, and Aviii verso.

12. This idea can be found echoed in the Renaissance proverbs about women and fools gathered by Le Roux de Lincy, *Le Livre des proverbes français* 1:219–32, 235–45. On the subject of popular attitudes toward women, see also Natalie Zemon Davis, *Society and Culture in Early Modern France* (Palo Alto, Calif.: Stanford University Press, 1975), 65–95, 124–51.

13. See the facsimile, *La Danse macabre des femmes*, Paris, 1977, fols. Av verso, Avii, Bi verso, Bii, Bii verso, Biii.

14. On parallel developments in literature, satirizing the merchant trades and the trait of avarice among the bourgeoisie, see Jean V. Alter, *Les Origines de la satire anti-bourgeoise en France. Moyen Age—XVIe siècle. Travaux d'humanisme et renaissance* 83 (Geneva: Droz, 1966), 26–40, 116–29.

15. On the subject of the co-existence of printed and manuscript books as well as exchanges between these two forms, see Curt Bühler, *The Fifteenth-Century Book: The Scribes, the Printers, the Decorators* (Philadelphia: University of Pennsylvania Press, 1960), and Sandra Hindman and James Douglas Farquhar, *Pen to Press: Illustrated Manuscripts and Printed Books in the First Century of Printing* (College Park, Md.: University of Maryland, Art Department, 1977).

16. On the costume of this period, see Jules Quicherat, *Histoire du costume en France depuis les temps les plus reculés jusqu'à la fin du XVIIIe siècle* (Paris: Librairie Hachette, 1875), 330–41, and Françoise Boucher, *Histoire du costume en occident de l'antiquité à nos jours*, 2d ed. (Paris: Flammarion, 1983), 191–217. I gratefully acknowledge the assistance of Anne van Buren, whose book on costume is forthcoming.

17. On European sumptuary laws, including the French versions, see Hermann Weiss, *Kostumkunde. Geschichte der Tracht und des Gerathes*, Band II, *Vom 4 bis 14 Jahrhundert* (Stuttgart: Verlag von Ebner & Seubert, 1872), 113. In France, the first sumptuary laws date from 1180 during the reign of Philip Augustus; additional clothing ordinances were passed in 1230, 1294, 1350, 1387, and 1400.

18. Julia Kalbfleisch, ed., *Le Triumphe des Dames von Olivier de la Marche*. There are seven manuscripts of the *Triumphe* or *Parement des Dames*; two are illustrated.

19. See the facsimile, *La Danse macabre des femmes*, fols. Aiiii, Aiiii verso, Bi verso, Avii verso.

20. Examples of this association abound and are even proverbial: "tomber en quenouille" was used to express the impossibility of the monarchy falling to the female line. See Jean Delumeau, *La Peur en Occident (XIVe–XVIIIe siècles)*, Une cité assiégée (Paris: Librairie Arthème Fayard, 1978), 340–45.

21. One of the first illustrated texts devoted to witchcraft was Ulric Molitor's *De Lamiis et Phitonicis Mulieribus* (Cologne: Cornelius von Zierikzee, 1489), discussed in *Europe in Torment, 1450–1550*, exh. cat., Brown University and the Rhode Island School of Design Museum

of Art (Providence, 1974), 62ff., and by Henry Charles Lea, *Materials Toward a History of Witchcraft*, 3 vols. (Philadelphia: University of Pennsylvania Press, 1939), and Delumeau, 305ff.

22. On the costumes of fools, see Enid Welsford, *The Fool, His Social and Literary History* (London: Faber and Faber, 1935), 118–19, and Barbara Swain, *Fools and Folly during the Middle Ages and the Renaissance* (New York: Columbia University Press, 1932), 84–89, with comments on the colors yellow and green. Anne van Buren states that the fool's garment is utterly fantastic, combining elements from men's dress, such as the traditional fool's chapperon, the *rochet* (an undergarment of fine lawn), and the outer gown with side slits in the skirt, like the conventional one for prophets and magicians.

23. See the facsimile, *La Danse macabre des femmes*, fols. Biv verso–Bvi. The third of these three images, that on fol. Bvi, was reused by Marchant to illustrate the shepherdesses Beatrix and Sebille on fol. Aiiii of the *Calendrier des bergères* (Paris, 1499), a copy of which is in BN, Rés. V. 1266. This edition of the *Calendrier* includes a reprint of the women's danse macabre, which begins on fol. Iiii.

24. A deluxe manuscript of this work, composed by a Franciscan, is in BN, Ms. fr. 147; it dates from approximately 1470 to 1480 and preserves the royal arms of France along with arms of the Dauphine and the house of Bourbon.

25. Kalbfleisch, *Le Triumphe des Dames*. Two manuscripts are illuminated: BN, MSS fr. 1848, 25431, the latter with an extensive cycle that depicts each item of clothing.

26. John Plummer, comp., *The Last Flowering*, no. 91, p. 70. Philippe's *Vita Christi* is in Lyons, Bib. Mun., Ms. 5125.

27. Plummer, *Last Flowering*, no. 91, pp. 66–71, 97–98. BN, Ms. fr. 702.

28. BN, Ms. lat. 14818 is, as far as I know, unpublished. I thank François Avril for calling it to my attention.

29. A seventeenth- or eighteenth-century inscription on fol. 1 identifies the manuscript as one in the library of St.-Victoire, and its shelf mark also appears in the manuscript. A miniature depicting Saint Victor strengthens the manuscript's association with the abbey.

30. Compare, for example, Ms. fr. 702, fol. 9, and Ms. fr. 995, fols. 1 verso, 2 verso, 4, 6, 6 verso, 28, 29, and 32.

31. Vienna, Österreichische Nationalbibliothek, Cod. 2625. On this manuscript, connected to the "School of Rouen," see Otto Pächt and Dagmar Thoss, *Die illuminierten Handschriften*, 1:81–84, figs. 58–59; 2: pls. 168–77.

32. Compare Ms. fr. 995, fols. 7 verso, 27 verso, and 38, with Cod. 2625, fols. 22, 10, and 31, respectively. Another manuscript, a Book of Hours sold at Sotheby's, also has borders identical to those in Ms. fr. 995. See Sotheby and Co., *Catalogue of Western Manuscripts and Miniatures*, 9 Dec. 1974, lot 63, 38–40, and compare fol. 170 with Ms. fr. 995, fol. 39 verso. A reproduction of fol. 170 is found in Pächt and Thoss, vol. 1, fig. 55.

33. Pächt and Thoss, 1:82. The Vienna manuscript, an allegory about Margaret of Austria's life, is probably the presentation copy made for her. On this group, with further bibliography, see also *Last Flowering*, 98.

34. The classic work remains A. Le Roux de Lincy, *La Vie d'Anne de Bretagne*. See also Jean Markale, *Anne de Bretagne*.

35. On Anne's library, which is thought to have contained as many as 1,300 to 1,500 volumes (although only forty-one manuscripts have been identified), see Michael Jones, "Les Manuscripts d'Anne de Bretagne, reine de France, duchesse de Bretagne," *Mémoires de la Société d'Histoire et d'Archéologie de Bretagne* 55 (1978), 43–81. Although Jones suggests that her collection may have become part of the royal

library at Blois after her death, he admits that we do not know what actually happened to it.

36. Le Roux de Lincy, *La Vie*, 2:35–36n. 1, and Joseph van Praet, *Catalogue des livres imprimés*, 5:160–61 (Rés. VV. H. 298 m).

37. A manuscript of this work that might be the presentation copy is now in Nantes, Musée Dobrée, Ms. 17. The description in the catalogue is by G. Durville, *Catalogue des manuscrits du Musée Dobrée* (Nantes: Musée Dobrée, 1904), 424–54, ed. G. Jeanneau and Antoine Dufour, *Les Vies des femmes célèbres* (Geneva: Librairie Droz, 1970). It was exhibited in Nantes, Musée Dobrée, *Anne de Bretagne et son temps* (Nantes, 1961), no. 76, p. 42, where the illuminations are said to recall the art of Jean Colombe and is listed in Jones, "Les Manuscrits," no. 14, p. 74.

38. Anne's copy, formerly in the Libri Collection, is thought to be lost; see Jones, no. 29, p. 77. A deluxe illuminated version of this work, dating from Anne's lifetime, is in BN, Ms. fr. 873.

39. Two manuscripts are extant: BN, MSS fr. 1952 and 1704. On this work, see H. Guy, *Histoire de la poésie française au XVIe siècle*, 2 vols. (Paris: H. Champion, 1968), 1:115. According to Jones, no. 34, p. 78, Anne's copy is said to be at BN, Ms. fr. 9225.

40. See Max Bruchet, *Marguerite d'Autriche, duchesse de Savoie* (Lille: Imprimerie L. Danel, 1927), as well as G. de Boom, *Marguerite d'Autriche-Savoie et la Pré-Renaissance* (Geneva: Droz, 1935).

41. This work, first printed in 1529 and translated into French in 1530, is discussed from the perspective of its connection with feminist literature by Emile V. Telle, *L'Oeuvre de Marguerite d'Angoulême Reine de Navarre et la Querelle des Femmes* (1937; reprint, Geneva: Slatkine Reprints, 1969), 45–55.

42. Vienna, Österreichische Nationalbibliothek, Cod. 3441. Pächt and Thoss, 1:87–91, pls. v, 186–95.

43. The inventory is published by M. Michelant, "Inventaire de la librairie de Marguerite d'Autriche, le 9 juillet, 1523," *Bulletin de la commission royale d'histoire de Belgique*, ser. 3, 22 (1871), 5–78, 83–136. See also the exhibition catalogue, which connects extant items with those in the inventory: *La Librairie de Marguerite d'Autriche*, M. Debae, comp. (Brussels: Bibliothèque Royale, 1987). Those items by Christine de Pizan, which include the *Cité des dames*, the *Livre des trois vertus*, and the *Livre des fais d'armes*, are found in the Michelant inventory, pp. 34, 40, 42.

44. See Marcel Francon, *Albums poétiques de Marguerite d'Autriche* (Cambridge, Mass.: Harvard University Press, 1934).

45. See H. P. Clive, *Marguerite de Navarre: An Annotated Bibliography* (London: Grant and Cutler, 1983); Marie Cerati, *Marguerite de Navarre* (Paris: Editions du Sorbier, 1981); and Telle, *L'Oeuvre de Marguerite*.

46. See Pierre Pradel, *Anne de France 1461–1522* (Paris: Editions Publisud, 1986), and the exhibition catalogue, *Anne de Beaujeu* (Lyon: Archives Départementales du Rhône, 1986); Hammerstein, 177–78.

47. A.-M. Chazaud, ed., *Les Enseignements d'Anne de France duchesse de Bourbonnais et d'Auvergne à sa fille Susanne de Bourbon* (Moulins: C. Desrosiers, 1878). The only manuscript of this work is in Leningrad. Chazaud publishes the inventories of Anne's and Susanne's libraries, which include many works by Christine de Pizan and Olivier de la Marche, as well as a manuscript copy of the danse macabre written on paper (pp. 213–58).

48. On her manuscripts, see Mary Beth Winn, "Books for a Princess and Her Son, Louise of Savoie, François d'Angoulême and the Parisian Libraire Antoine Verard," *Bibliothèque d'Humanisme et Renaissance* 46 (1984), 603–17, and Myra Dickman Orth, "Francis DuMoulin and Louise of Savoy," *The Sixteenth Century Journal* 13 (1982), 55–66.

49. See M.-F. Castelain, *Au Pays de Claude de France* ([Romorantin]: Société d'Art, d'histoire et d'archéologie de Sologne, 1986). On her manuscript Books of Hours, see C. Sterling, *The Master of Claude Queen of France, a Newly Defined Miniaturist* (New York: H. P. Kraus, 1975), and Castelain, color plate opposite p. 14 of Cambridge, Fitzwilliam Museum, Ms. 159. Her *Livre du Sacré* is in BN, Ms. 5750.

Le mort

Tantoſt naures vaillant ce pic
Des biens du mõde et de nature
Eueſque: de vous il eſt pic
Non oſtant voſtre prelature.
Voſtre fait giet en auenture.
De vous ſubges fault rẽdꝛe cõpte:
A chaſcun dien ſera dꝛoiture.
Neſt pas aſſeur q̃ trop hault mõte

Leueſque

Le ceur ne me peul eſioir
Des nouuelles que moꝛt mapoꝛte.
Dieu vouldꝛa de tout compte oir:
Ceſt ce que plus me deſconfoꝛte.
Le monde auſſi peu me conforte:
Qui tous a la fin deſherite.
Il retient tout: nul rien nempoꝛte.
Tout ce paſſe foꝛs le merite.

Le mort

Auancez vous gent eſcuier
Qui ſaues de danſer les tours.
Lance poꝛties: et eſcu hier:
Et huy vous fineres vos iours
Il neſt rien qui ne pꝛaigne cours.
Danſez: et panſez de ſuir.
Vous ne pouez auoir ſecours.
Il neſt qui moꝛt puiſſe fuir.

Leſcuier

Puis que moꝛt me tient en ſes las
Aumois que ie puiſſe vng mot dire
Adieu deduis: adieu ſolas:
Adieu dames: plus ne puis rire.
Penſez de lame qui deſire
Repos. ne vous chaille plus tant
Du coꝛps: que tꝰ leſiours empire.
Tous fault moꝛir on ne ſcet quant

Fig. 1. The Bishop and the Constable, *Danse macabre* (Paris: Guy Marchant, 1485), Grenoble, Bibliothèque Municipale, Incun. 327.

Ergo time. te instrue . corrige mentem. viue mori presto : debita ferre para.
Dum licet et spacium datur : ista resinque pro patria celi. qua sine fine dies.

La mort.

Apres : nouuelle mariee
Qui auez mis voftre defir
A danfer : z eftre paree
Pour feftes z nopces choifir
En danfant ie vous vien faifir
Au iourduy ferez mife en terre
Mort ne vient iamais a plaifir
Joye fen va comme feu de ferre

La nouuelle mariee

Las : demy an entier na pas
Que comence a tenir mefnage
Par quoy fi toft paffer le pas
Né my eft pas doulceur : mais raige
Jauoye defir en mariage
De faire mons et merueilles
Mais la mort detrop pres me charge
Ung peu de vent abat grant fueilles

La mort.

Femme groffe prenez loifir
Denfendre a vous legierement
Car huy mourrez ceft le plaifir
De dieu z fon commandement
Allons pas a pas bellement
En gettant voftre cueur es cieulx
Et nayes peur aucunement
Dieu ne fait rien que pour le mieulx

La femme groffe

Jauray bien petit de deduit
De mon premier enfantement
Si recommande a dieu le fruit
Et mon ame pareillement
Helas : bien cuidoye autrement
Auoir grant ioye en ma gefine
Mais tout va bien piteufement
Fortune toft fe change z fine

Fig. 2. The Newlywed and the Pregnant Wife, *Grant danse macabre des femmes* (Paris: Guy Marchant, 1491), Paris, Bibliothèque Nationale, Rés. Ye. 86, fol. Avii.

Omnium mortalium cura quis multiplicium studiorum labor exerceat diuerso
quidem calle ad vnum tamen beatitudinis finem nititur peruenire Boetius

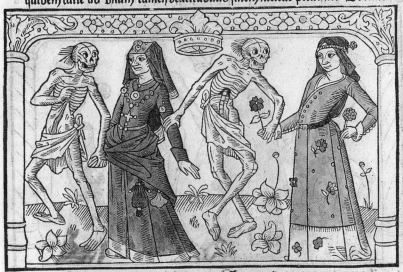

La mort

Approuches vous reuenderesse
Sans plus cy faire demouree
Voftre corps: nuyt et iour ne cesse.
De gaigne r pour estre honnouree.
Honneur est de poure duree.
Et se part en vng momét deure
Au monde na chose asseuree
Tel rit au matin qui au soir pleure.

La reuenderesse

Jauoie hier gaignie deux escus
Pour sourfaire subtilement:
Mais ne scay qui les ma tollus
Argent acquis mauuesement
Ne fait ia bien communement
Helas ie meurs cest dautre metz.
Que prestre aye hatiuement
Car il vault mieulx tart qiamais

La mort

Femme de petite value
Mal viuant en charnalite
Mene aues vie dissolue
Entous temps puer et este
Aies le cueur espouente.
Car vous seres de pres tenue
Pour mal faire on est tourmente
Pechie nuit quant on continue

La femme amoureuse.

A ce pechie me suis soubzmise
Pour plaisance desordonnee
Pedus solét ceulx qui my ont mise
Et au mestier habandonnee
Las se ieusse estoy bien menee.
Et conduite premierement
Jamais ny eusse estoy tournee.
La fin suyt le commencement.

b ii.

Fig. 3. The Resaleswoman and the Prostitute, *Grant danse macabre des femmes*
(Paris: Guy Marchant, 1491), Paris, Bibliothèque Nationale, Rés. Ye. 86, fol. Bii.

La mort

Femme daccueil et amiable
A festier gens a plante:
Acquis auez amis de table
Pour parler de ioyeusete:
Le temps nest tel quil a este
Rien ne vault icy vacabont
Parler: qui nest que vanite
Ceulx qui ont le bruit ont le bont

La femme daccueil

Auiourduy parens et amis
Promettet et mons et merueilles
Mais quãt voiēt quõ est bas mis
Ilz baillent frettous les oreilles
Et sont aussi sours cõme fueilles
Que le vēt fait voler par couples
Et que vallent promesses telles
Vrais ne sõt pas les amis doubles

La mort

Apres nourrice: vostre beau filz
Monobstant son couuertouer
Et son beau bonnet a trois filz
Vous ne le menrez plus iouer
Deslogez vous sans delaier
Car tous deux vo⁹ mourrez ensēble
Vous ne poues plus cy targer
La mort prēt tout quãt bõ luy sēble

La nourrice

A ceste danse fault aler
Comme sont les prestres au seyne
Je voulsisse bien reculer
Mais ie me sēs la boce en laine
Entre les bras: de mon alaine
Cest enfãt meurt depidimie.
Cest grãt pitie de mort soudaine
Il nest qui ait heure ne demie

Fig. 4. The Hostess and the Wetnurse, *Grant danse macabre des femmes* (Paris: Guy Marchant, 1491), Paris, Bibliothèque Nationale, Rés. Ye. 86, fol. Aviii verso.

Non eſt iſta dies curſus Vt iſta. Dierum
Eſt deus iſta dies. Vltima noſtra quies

La mort.

Dictes ieune femme a la cruche
Renommee bonne chamberiere
Respondez au moins quāt on huche
Sans tenir si rude maniere
Vous nires plus a la riuiere
Bauer:au four na la feneſtre
Ceſt cy voſtre iournee derniere
Auſli toſt meurt seruant que maiſtre

La chamberiere

Quoy:ma maiſtreſſe ma promis
Me marier z des biens faire
Et puis si ay dautres amys
Qui luy aideront a parfaire
He:men iray ie sans riens faire
Jen appelle on me fait tort
Auſli ne men ſcauroye taire
Peu de gens deſirent la mort

La mort.

Scauez vous recōmanderreſſe
Point vng bon lieu pour moy loger:
Jay bien meſtier que on madreſſe
Car nul ne me veult heberger
Mais ien feray tant deſloger
Que on congnoiſtra mon enseigne
Mourir fault pour vous abreger
Nul ne pert que autre ne gaigne

La recommāderreſſe

En la mort na point damitie
Et si ne fait riens pour requeſte
Or argent priere pitie
Pour neant on sen font la teſte
Qui y veult reſiſter eſt beſte
La mort a nully ne complaiſt
Et fault tous danſer a la feſte
Mourir cōuient quant a dieu plaiſt

Fig. 5. The Chambermaid and the Hosteler, *Grant danse macabre des femmes* (Paris: Guy Marchant, 1491), Paris, Bibliothèque Nationale, Rés. Ye. 86, fol. Avii verso.

Ley metuenda premit mortales. omnibus vna Mors cita sed dubia.
nec fugienda Venit. Circuit et sui gens sol Vitam prestat. et item,
Cum cadit annichillat quod nichil ante fuit. Sic dat. sic retrahit.
iterum trahet. atqz retrapit Omnia. sol girans quod dedit. ipse trahit

Lacteur.

Mirez vous icy mirez femmes
Et mettes vostre affection
A penser a voz poures ames
Qui desirent saluacion
Cy bas nest pas la mansion
On vous deuez estre tousiours
Mort met tout a destruction
Grãt z petit meurt tous les iours

Pour noblesse ne pour honneur
Pour richesse ou pourete
Pour estre dame de valeur
Ou femme de mendicite
Ne differe mort equite:
Mais autant dune part q dautre
Sans auoir mercy ne pite
Huy prẽt lune:et demain lautre

a.ii.

Fig. 6. Authority, *Grant danse macabre des femmes* (Paris: Guy Marchant, 1491), Paris, Bibliothèque Nationale, Rés. Ye. 86, fol. Aii.

Quid fetidius humano cadauere. quid horribilius femina mortua Cuius gratissimus erat amplexus in Vita molestus erit eciam aspectus in morte

La mort
Suyues mon train religieuse
De voz fais conuient rendre compte
Se point nauez estez piteuse
Aux poures: ce vous sera honte
En paradis point on ne monte
Fors par degrez de charite
Entendes bien a voftre compte
Tout ce quon fait y eft compte

La religieuse
Jay fait par tout ce que iay peu
Aux poures selon leur venue
Les malades pense: et repeu
Non si bien que iestoye tenue
Mais se faulte il eft aduenue
Dieu me pardonne la defaille
Sa grace tousiours retenue
Il neft si iufte qui ne faille

La mort
Oyez oyez: ou vous fait fauoir
Que cefte vieille forciere
A fait mourir et deceuoir
Plusieurs gés en mainte maniere
Eft condamnee comme meurtriere
A mourir: ne diura plus gaire
Je la maine en fon cymitiere
Ceft belle chofe de bien faire

La forciere
Mes bonnes gens ayes pitie
De moy: et toute pechereffe
Et me donnes par amitie
Don de patenoftre ou de meffe
Jay fait du mal en ma ieuneffe
Dont icy achete la prune
Si pries dieu que lame adreffe
Qui ne peult contre fa fortune
b. iii:

Fig. 7. The Nun and the Witch, *Grant danse macabre des femmes* (Paris: Guy Marchant, 1491), Paris, Bibliothèque Nationale, Rés. Ye. 189, fol. Biii.

Si quis sentiret qus tendit et vnde veniret
Nuq̃ gauderet sed omni tempore fleret

La mort

Dieu ayme bien femes deuotes
Qui ont consciences nettes
Et hait sur toutes ses bigotes
Aux chaperons sans cornetes
Côme autunes leurs coletes
Lesquelles par ypocrisie
En secretz pechez sont infertes
Denant dieu et sa compaignie

La bigote

Pour verite me suis monstree
Souuent meilleur que ie nestoye
Aucunefops bien desieunee
Faisant seblant que ie ie ynoye
Et de ma bouche barbetoye
Sans dire ne mot ne lettre
Je pry a dieu quen bonne voye
Plaise ma poure ame mettre

La mort

Sus tost margot venez auant
Estez vous maintenaut derriere
Vous deuffiez ia estre dauant
Et danser toute la premiere
Quel contenãce: quel maniere
Ou est vostre fille marote
Ne vault faire cy maigre chiere
Car cest vostre derniere note

La sotte

Entre vous coinctes et iolies
Femme oyez que ie vous dis
Laiffez a heure voz folies
Car vous mourres sãs contredis
Si iay meffait ne mesdis
A ceulx qui demeurent: pardon
Requiero: et a dieu paradis
Demãder ne puis plus beau don

Fig. 8. The Hypocrite and the Fool, *Grant danse macabre des femmes* (Paris: Guy Marchant, 1491), Paris, Bibliothèque Nationale, Rés. Ye. 189, fol. Biii verso.

Fig. 9. Death of King Darius and Capture of Cyrus, Xenophon, *Cyropaedia*, Paris, Bibliothèque Nationale, Ms. fr. 702, fol. 9 recto.

Fig. 10. Nativity, Missal of St. Victoire, Paris, Bibliothèque Nationale, Ms. lat. 14818, fol. 23 verso.

Fig. 11. Margaret of Austria, in Michel Ritz, *Changement de Fortune en toute prosperité*, Vienna, Österreichische Nationalbibliothek, Cod. 2625, fol. 31.

The Manuscript

Ludite formose teneres cantate puelle
Nam defluunt anni more fluentis aque
Nec que preteriit iterum revocabitur unda
Nec que preteriit hora redire potest

Le premier menestrier

1 Venez dames et damoiselles
Du siecle et de religion
Veufes mariees et pucelles
Et autres sans exception
De quelconques condition
Toutes dancer a ceste dance
Vous y venrez vueillez ou non
8 Qui sage est souvent pense

Le second

9 Quelz sont voz corps ie vous demande
Femmes iolyes tant bien paree
Ilz sont pour certain la viande
Quun iour sera aux vers donnee
Des vers sera donc devoree
Vostre cher qui est fresche et tendre
Ja il nen demoura goulee
16 Voz vers apres deviendront cendre.

Make merry, sing out beautiful young maidens,
For the years run down like a flowing stream.
The waters which have passed will not return
Nor can the hour which has gone come back.

The First Musician

1 Come mesdames and mesdemoiselles,
From world and cloister
Widows, brides, and virgins,
And others without exception,
Whatever your condition
You all will dance in this Dance.
Like it or no you will come to it.
8 Whoever is wise thinks of this often.

The Second

9 What are your bodies, I ask you,
Pretty women, so well dressed?
They are surely meat
Which one day will be given to worms
Then by worms devoured.
Of your flesh which is fresh and tender
Not even a mouthful will remain.
16 Afterward your worms will turn to ashes.

NOTES: The Latin lines found in B.N.fr. 995 serve a decorative and moralizing function. Most of them are taken from the 1486 printed edition where they appeared in quatrains at the top of the pages.

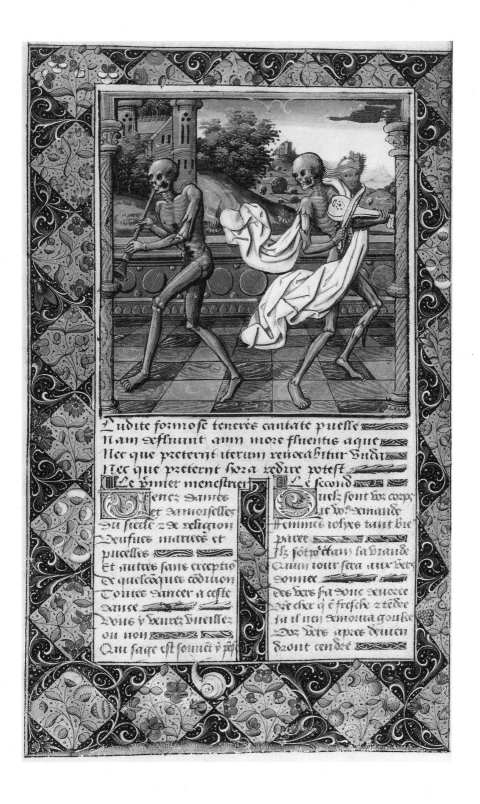

Lines 1–8. The First Musician uses several terms to call female readers: *dames, demoiselles, veuves, mariees, pucelles*. The first two designate women of the upper classes, *demoiselle* limited

Le tiers

1 Compaignon bonne est ta raison
De ces femmes oultre cuydee
Que leurs corps sera venaison
De vers puans ung iour mengee
Et pourroient elles estre gardee
Pour or argent ne riens qui soit
Nenny bien sont donc ques abusee
8 Qui ne s'amende il se decoit

Le quart

9 Femmes mirez vous en ung tas
Dossemens de gens trespassez
Lesquelz ont en divers estatz
Au monde este leurs temps passez
Et maintenant sont entassez
Lun sur lautre gros et menus
Ainsi serez or y pensez
16 La chair pourrie les os tous nudz

The Third

1 Comrade, your thought is good
About these presumptious women,
For their bodies will be game
Eaten one day by putrid worms.
And could they be preserved
For gold, silver, or any other thing?
No, no. Many there are who are mistaken.
8 Whoever mends not his ways deceives himself.

The Fourth

9 Women, imagine yourselves in a heap
Of bones from people who have died,
Who have filled many worldly roles
In their time past
And [who] now are piled
One on the other, fat and thin,
So you will be, think of that now,
16 Rotted flesh, bones all bare.

---

to unmarried and generally young ladies. *Veuve, mariee,* and *pucelle* represent stages in marital life, presented in reverse chronological order, or in order of their closeness to the event of death: widow, bride, virgin.

NOTES: *Line 9.* The Second, Third, and Fourth Musicians and Authority, who follows them, prefer the general term *femmes* to address the audience. *Femmes* is flexible enough to be appropriate for women of many social ranks, several types of marital status, and a range of ages; it conveys neither a tone of social condescension (as English "woman" sometimes can) nor biological coldness (as English "female").

For a full discussion of the Musicians of Death and their functions see Reinhold Hammerstein, *Tanz und Musik des Todes,* especially pp. 73–74.

Grisay, Lavis, and Dubois-Stasse (*Les Dénominations de LA FEMME*) claim that *femme* is never used for direct address (709). In the *Danse Macabre des Femmes,* that is clearly not the case, as this folio shows.

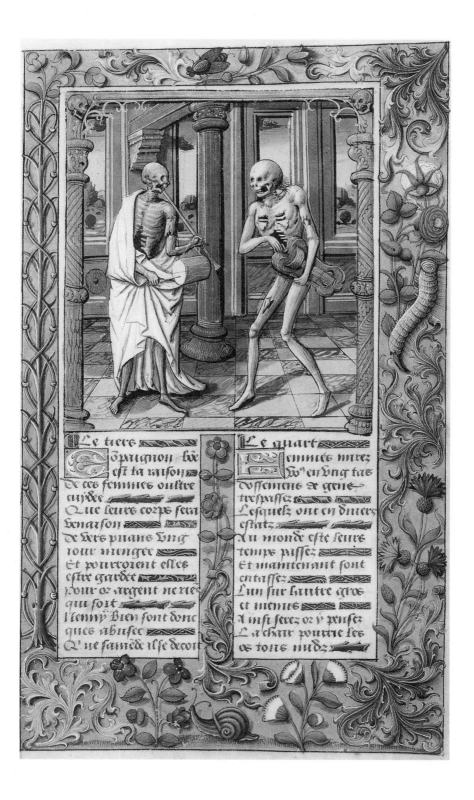

Le tiers

Compaignon bõ
est ta raison
de ces femmes oultre
cuijdee
Que leurs corps seront
benarson
de Vers puans Vng
tour mengee
Et pourroient elles
estre gardee
pour or argent ne riens
qui soit
Nenny Bien sont donc
ques abusee
Que sainct il se decoit

Le quart

Femmes mirez
Vous en Vng tas
dossement de gent
trespasse
Lesquelz ont en diuers
estatz
Au monde este leurs
temps passez
Et maintenant sont
entasse
Lun sur laultre gros
et menue
Ainsi serez or y pensez
La chair pourrie les
os tous nudz

L'acteur

1 Mirez vous cy hommes et femmes
Et mettez vostre affection
A penser a voz povres ames
Qui desirent salvation
Cy bas nest pas la mansion
Ou vous devez estre tousiours
Mort met tout a destruction
8 Grant et petit meurt tous les iours

9 Pour noblesse ne pour honneur
Pour richesses ou povrete
Pour porter estat de valleur
Ou du tout de mendiate
Ne dissere mort equite
Mais autant dune part que dautre
Sans avoir mercy ne pitie
16 Huy prent lung et demain lautre

24 VERSO
Translation

Authority

1 Look here, men and women,
And turn your hearts
To think of your poor souls
Which desire salvation.
Here on earth is not your home
Where you should stay forever.
Death destroys everything.
8 Great and small die every day.

9 Neither for nobility nor honor
Nor wealth nor poverty
Nor high estate
Nor beggarliness
Will Death renounce equality.
But as often from one quarter as from another,
Merciless, pitiless Death
16 Takes one today, another tomorrow.

NOTES: *Role name. Acteur* is a common Middle French term derived from a confusion of Latin *actorem* (agent) and *auctorem* (authority, respected author). It does not signify a dramatic actor. In A, the text immediately preceding the *Danse Macabre* is called the *Dance aux aveugles*. It consists of a series of dance poems *(Dance Cupido, Dance de Fortune, Dance de la Mort)*, and throughout a figure called Acteur appears so regularly as to be a major source of unity in the work. Acteur opens the whole ensemble with eight-line stanzas (the same poetic form as is found in this text) and offers prose statements at the beginning and end of each of the three principal segments. A similar figure occurs throughout the *Histoire et Plaisante Chronique du petit Jehan de Saintré* by Antoine de La Sale, dated around 1456. Thus, Acteur was fully developed outside of and prior to the first attested appearance of either the danse macabre of men or of women, and his function in this poem was expanded in each subsequent version.

Ex utero natis posita est lex ire: sed esse
Certos: sub sole perpetuare nichil

La mort

1 Noble royne de beau corsage
Gente et ioyeuse a ladvenant
Jay de par le grant maistre charge
De vous en mener maintenant
Et comme chose bien advenant
Cest dance commencerez
Faictes devoir au remanant
8 Vous qui vivez ainsi ferez

La royne

9 Cest dance mest bien nouvelle
Et en ay le cueur bien surpris
He Dieu quelle dure nouvelle
A gens qui ne lont pas apris
Las en la mort est tout compris
Royne dame grant ou petite
Les plus grans sont les premiers pris
16 Contre la mort na point de fuite

To all born of the womb is fixed a bitter law
And of this be certain, nothing under the sun is lasting

Death

1 Noble Queen of handsome form,
Comely and blithe in bearing,
I am charged by the Grand Master
To lead you now,
And as is fitting,
You will begin this dance.
Do your duty to those who follow.
8 According to the life you lead, you shall behave.

The Queen

9 This dance is very new to me,
My heart is overcome by it.
Oh God, what cruel news
For those who haven't learned it yet.
Alas! In Death each one is taken up,
Queen, each lady, high or low.
The grandest are the first ones seized.
16 There is no flight away from death.

NOTES: The Queen, dressed in a crimson robe trimmed with the ermine befitting royalty, also wears several gold chains and a crown. She is reminded of her duties as a leader, and as she attests to the leveling power of Death, she reinforces the strict protocol of the dance in which the greatest must come first.

In the printed editions of the poem, each live woman is addressed by a dead woman (labeled *la Morte*); here, it is Death, *la Mort*, who calls each participant.

Ex utero natis pedetentim calle sub ipso
Subdola mors comes est nos laqueare studens

La mort

1 Apres madame la duchesse
Vous viens querir et pourchasser
Ne pensez plus a la richesse
A biens na ioyaulx a masser
Auiourdhuy vous fault trespasser
Pourquoy de vostre vie est fait
Folie est de tant embrasser
8 On nemporte que le bien fait

La duchesse

9 Je nay pas encor trente ans
Helas a l'heure qui commance
A savoir que cest de bon temps
Mort me vient tollir ma plaisance
Jay des amys a grant chevance
Soulas esbatz gens a devis
Pourquoy mome me plaist ceste dance
16 Gens aises si meurent en vie

From the mother's womb on, stealthy death is a constant
  companion
Seeking to ensnare us, on our very path

Death

1 And next, Madame Duchess,
I come to seek and find you.
Think no more of riches
Or amassing goods or jewels.
Today you must die,
Because your life is over.
It is madness to covet so much.
8 All one takes away is the deed well done.

The Duchess

9 I am not yet thirty.
Alas, when I am just beginning
To know what a good time really is,
Death comes to take away my pleasure.
I have such important friends,
Delights, amusements, such fun people,
That's why the dance is so displeasing to me.
16 Wealthy people die thus, in mid life.

Ex utero natis pedetentim passe sub ipso
Subdola mors comes est nos laqueare studens

La mort

Apres madame
la duchesse
vous viens querir et
pourchasser
Ne pese plus, la richesse
A biens na tourdulx a
masser
Aniourdhuy vo fault
trespasser
Pourquoy de vostre vie
est fait
folie est de tant embasser
On nemporte que
le bien fait

La duchesse

Ie nay pas encor
trente ans
Helas, a leure que comace
A savoir que est de
bon temps
Mort me vient tollir
ma pluisance
Iay de amis a grant
cheuance
Soulas estoit gens de
renne
Pourquoy moms me
plaist ceste dance
Gens assez si meurent en

Passibus invigilat nostris mors omnia rodens
Nec finit esse diu, quicquid in orbe fluit

La mort

1 Or ca madame la regente
Qui avez renom de bien dire
De dancer fringuer estre gente
Sur toutes qu'on sauroit eslire
Vous souliez autres faire rire
Festier gens et ralier
Or est il temps de vous reduire
8 La mort fait trestot oublier

La regente

9 Quant me souvient des tabourins
Nopces festes harpes trompettes
Menestrelz doulceines clarins
Et des grans cheres iay faictes
Je cognois que telz entrefaictes
En temps de mort nont point de lieu
Maiz tornent en povres emplaites
16 Tot se passe fors aymer dieu

Death watches our steps gnawing all away
Nor will it cease as long as anything on earth endures

Death

1 Now then, Madame Regent,
Renowned for good conversation,
For dancing, playing, being pleasant,
Above all women one might choose
You had the habit of making others laugh,
Making people happy, bringing them together.
Now it is time to lead you out.
8 Death makes us soon forget.

The Regent

9 When I remember the tambourines,
Weddings, parties, harps, trumpets,
Musicians, oboes, clarions,
And the grand feasts I have made,
I realize that such affairs
Have no place in time of death,
But turn into bad bargains.
16 All fades away save loving God.

NOTES: *Role Names.* Most dictionaries of the sixteenth century define the word *regente* in political terms, a lady governing or ruling. Here the Regent's activities seem restricted to those of a hostess.

G shows *Femme de Chevalier* as the name for the Regent, and *Arogente* as the name for the Knight's Lady.

Passibus iungisat nris mors omnia roxens
Ne simt esse diu quicquid in orbe fluit

La mort

r ca madame
la regente
Qui auez renom & bie
aire
De dancer frinquer estu
regente
Sur toutes quo sauroi
estue
vous souliez autres fai
re raue
Festier gens & rasier
Or est il temps de vous
reduire
La mort fait tresso* oublier

La regente

Quant me sou
uient des talou
rms
Nopxes festes harpes
trompettes
Menestrelz doulceines
charmis
Et des grant cheres tar
fuictes
Je congnois q tel estresitez
En téps de mort nont poit
& lieu
marz tonet exoutes explaiteq
To* se passe fort armer dieu

Continuo cadimus viventes filia sororum
Atropos arrumpens emula sepe venit

La mort

1 Gentille femme de chevalier
   Qui tant aymez deduit de chasse
   Que tost vous fault deshabiller
   Et suivre le train de ma trasse
   Cest bien chasse quant on pourchasse
   Chose a son ame meritoire
   Car au derrain mort tout enchasse
8 Cest vie est moult transitoire

La femme du chevalier

9 Pas si tost mourir ne cuidoye
   Et comment dea ie souppe hier
   Sus lerbe verte a la saulsoye
   Ou fis mon esprevier gayer
   En riens plus ne se fault fier
   Et quest ce des faitz de ce monde
   Huy rire demain lermoyer
16 La fin de ioye en dueil redonde

Oft comes the jealous sister Atropos to cut the thread
And forthwith we descend yet alive

Death

1 Genteel wife of the chevalier,
   Who love the joy of the hunt so much,
   Quickly you must get out of your gear
   And follow the retinue of my train.
   The hunting is good when one pursues
   Something worthwhile for one's soul,
   For in the end death hunts us all down.
8 This life is very fleeting.

The Knight's Lady

9 I did not think to die so soon.
   Just yesterday I had my supper
   On the green grass by the willow tree,
   Where I let my sparrow hawk play.
   We can't count on anything anymore.
   And what of the things of this world?
   Today we laugh, tomorrow we cry.
16 The end of joy is drowned in grief.

Continuo cadimus biuentes filia fororum[s]
A tropos arrumpene emula fepe bent

La mort

[G]entille femme
de cheualier
Qui tant aymez deduit
de chaffe
Vus toft vous fault
defhabiller
Et fuiure le train & ma
traffe
Ceft bien chaffe quant
on pourchiffe
Chofe a fo'amie meritoire
Car au derrain mort
tout enchaffe
Cefte vie e moult tifitoire

La femme du chlr

[H]a fi toft mou
rir ne cuidoye
Et comment dea ie foup
pe hier
Vus feele verte a La
fauffoye
Ou fis mon efpreuier
gaifer
En riés pl'ne fe fault fier
Et queft ce de faitz de
ce monde
Huy rar dmai fermoye
La fin de rofe en bueil
redonde

Fluctibus aut morbo seu flammis strage veneno
Macra fames calidum frigora cura nocent

La mort

1 Dame abesse vous laisseres
Labbaye quavez bien aymee
Quun peu de bien n'en porterez
Plus nen serez dame appellee
Vostre crosse dargent doree
Une de vos seurs portera
Qui apres vous sera sacree
8 Tout fut autruy tout y sera

Labesse

9 Le service hier ie fasoye
En leglise comme abbesse
Et ma crosse d'argent portoye
A matines et a la messe
Et auiourduy fault que ie lesse
Abbaye crosse et convent
He Dieu de ce monde questce
16 On est de mort surprise souvent

27 RECTO
Translation

Gaunt hunger, heat, cold and want bring harm
With floods or disease, by flames or famine or venom

Death

1 My Lady Abbess, you will leave
The abbey you have loved so well
Taking only a little goodness
[You] will never again be called My Lady.
Your cross of silver and of gold
One of your sisters now will wear.
After you she will be anointed.
8 Everything belonged to others, everything will stay there.

The Abbess

9 Yesterday I performed the service
As Abbess in the church
And I wore my silver cross
At Matins and at Mass,
And today I must leave
Abbey, cross, and convent.
Oh! God, what is this world?
16 One is often surprised by death.

Fluctibus aut morbo seu flammis strage veneno.
Aucta fames calidum frigora cura nocent.

La mort
Dame abesse vo'
laisseres
L abbaye quaues bien
aymee
Qui un peu de bien ne
porteres
Plus nen seres dame
appellee
Vre crosse argent doree
Que de vo' seurs por
tera
Qui apres vo' sera sacree
Tout fut auleur tout
y sera

L abesse
Le service hier
ne fasoye
En leglise comme ab
besse
Et ma crosse darget
portoye
A matines et ala messe
Et auiourduy fault q̄
re lesse
Abbaye crosse et couuent
Se bien de ce monde
quest ce
On est de mort surpris
souuent

Ergo quis in tantis possit cras dicere vivam
Cum videat quotiens mors male visa ferit

La mort

1 Dames plorez vos gorgerettes
  Il nest plus temps de vous farder
  Voz torteretz fronteaulx et bavettes
  Ne vous pourrovent icy aider
  Plusieurs sont deceuz par cuider
  Que la mort pour leur habit fleche
  Chascun y deust bien regarder
8 Par habit mainte femme peche

La femme de lescuier

9 He: Quay ie meffait ou mesdit
  Dont doyve souffrir telle perte
  Javoye achete au lendit
  Du drap pour taindre en escarlete
  Et eusse eu une robe verte
  Au premier iour de lan qui vient
  Mais mon emprise est descouverte
16 Tout ce quon pense pas nasdvient

Therefore who can expect to be alive on the morrow
When she realizes how often death strikes unawares

Death

1 Ladies, weep for your dressy collars.
  There is no more time to put on your rouge.
  Your muffs, your caps, and even your fillets
  Can not help you now.
  Many are deceived in thinking
  Death may yield to their [fair] dress.
  Each one should reflect with care:
8 Many a woman sins by her dress.

The Squire's Lady

9 Oh! What have I said or done
  To suffer such a loss.
  At the St. Denis Fair I had bought
  Cloth to dye scarlet
  And would have had a green gown
  For next New Year's Day,
  But my project is uncovered.
16 Not everything we expect comes to pass.

NOTES: *Line 11.* The *lendit,* one of Europe's oldest continuing annual fairs, was founded by King Dagobert (A.D. 629–39). Held in the plain of St. Denis, north of Paris, from June 11–24, it had become a fair emphasizing textiles by the late medieval period.

Ergo quis i tantis possit eras dicere buiam
Cum videat quotiens morte male visa ferit

La mort

Iames ploiez voz
gorgerettes
il nest plus temps de
vous farder
voz torterez fronteaulx
et barrettes
Ne vous pourroiet icy aider
Plusieurs sont deceuz
par cuider
Que la mort pour leur
habit flecle
Chascun y eust bien
regarder
par habit mainte femme

La femme de lesauter
ce quar ce messau
Dou mesdit
dont doine souffrir
telle perte
Ianore achete au lendit
du drap pour taindre
en escarlete
et eusse une robe verte
au premier tour de lan
qui vient
Mais mon emprise
est desconuerte
Tout ce quon pense
pas naduient

Non licet ut videor vane confidere vite
            In qua nulla fides est nisi certa mors

La mort

1 Se vous avez sans fiction
   Tout vostre temps servy a dieu
   Du cueur en la religion
   Laquelle vous avoit vestue
   Celuy qui tous biens retribue
   Vous compensera loyaument
   A son vouloir en temps et lieu
8 Bien fait requiert bon payement

La prieure

9 Jestoit en ma religion
   Servir a dieu tout mon desir
   En cloistre par devotion
   Dire mes heures a loisir
   Or mest venu la mort saisir
   Au monde nay point de regre
   Face dieu de moy son plaisir
16 Prendre doit on la mort en gre

One can not seem to put trust in barren life
            In which there is no certainty, but certain death

Death

1 If you really have given
   All your time to God,
   Your heart to the faith
   Which had enfolded you,
   He who rewards all good works
   Will compensate you faithfully
   According to His will, His time and place.
8 A good deed demands fair payment.

The Prioress

9 I was [at home] in my vocation;
   My whole desire to serve God
   Through devotion in the cloister,
   Reciting my Hours at my leisure.
   Now Death has come to take me.
   I do not regret the world.
   May God do with me as He pleases.
16 We must receive Death gratefully.

Non licet ut video sanc considere vite
In qua nulla fides est nisi certa mori

La mort **La prieure**

E vous auez
sans fiction
Tout vostre temps suy
a dieu
Du cueur en la religion
Laquelle vous auoit
vestue
Celuy qui tous biens
retribue
Vo° copenseca lognuit
A son vouloir en temp
et lieu
Bien fait requiert lo
payement

Iestout en ma
religion
Seruir a dieu tout mo
iesur
En cloistre p deuotion
Due mes heures a lorsir
Or mest venu la mort
saisir
Au monde nay point
de regre
Face dieu de moy son
plaisir
Prendre soit on La
mort en gre

Finge qui aspicias morientem sed freme namque
Consimili pena te vocat una dies

La mort

1 Venez apres ma damoiselle
Et serrez tous voz affiquetz
Nenchault se estes laide ou belle
Laisser vous fault plait et quaquetz
Plus ne irez a ces banquetz
Ou on sent si souef laue rose
Ne verrez iouster a roquetz
8 Femmes font faire molt de chose

Le damoiselle

9 Que me vallent mes grans atours
Mes habitz ieunesse beaulte
Quant tout me fault laisser en plours
Oultre mon gre et voulente
Mon corps sera tantost porte
Aux vers et a la pourriture
Plus nen sera balle ne chante
16 Joye mondaine bien peu dure

Dissemble, who sees someone dying, but tremble withal
For a similar fate will call you some day

Death

1 Come along, my Debutante,
And put away all your brooches.
It doesn't matter if you are ugly or fair.
You must leave the talk and chatter;
And go no more to banquets,
Where you smell sweet rose cologne.
You won't watch them jousting.
8 Women are the cause of many things.

The Debutante

9 What are they to me, my headdresses,
My clothing, youth, beauty,
When I must leave it all in tears.
Against my wishes, against my will,
Soon my body will be taken
To the worms and to decay.
No more dancing, no more singing,
16 Worldly pleasure scarcely lasts.

NOTES: This damoiselle is a Debutante, called by Death in the midst of her courtship season. She has danced, sung, attended banquets and other social gatherings, and behind it all lay the competition of her suitors, hinted at in Death's comment about her watching the jousting. Her youth, beauty, jewelry and clothing, and social graces were all-important assets for her future, only to be cast aside irrevocably at a moment's notice.

Line 6. Death's reference to rosewater (laue rose) has a double meaning since it was commonly used at funerals to freshen the air.

Est brevis illa dies hodie: quia forte dierum
Est michi sola dies: Heu metuenda dies

La mort

1 Et vous aussi gente bourgoise
Pourneant certes vous excusez
Il est force que chascun voise
Comme voyez et advisez
Voz beaulx gorgias empesez
Ny font rien ne large saincture
Maintz hommes en sont abusez
8 En tous estatz il fault mesure

La bourgoisse

9 Mes getz et colletz de letisses
Ne me exemptent point de mort
Mais mes grans ioyes et delices
Me viennent icy a remort
Ma conscience fort me mort
De folies faictes en ieunesse
Qui me sont a rebours tresfort
16 Joye en la fin tourne en tristesse

29 RECTO
Translation

Brief is this day today for it is perhaps for me
The only one, how fearful a day!

Death

1 You too, spruce townswoman,
Surely you are not escaping
Everyone must go.
As you see me and consider,
Your beautiful starched shirt front
And broad belt make no difference.
Many men are wrong about that.
8 In all things one needs moderation.

The Townswoman

9 My fillets and my ermine collars
Don't exempt me from Death.
But my great joys and delights
Now make me remorseful.
My conscience pricks
For youthful follies
Now gone completely sour.
16 In the end joy turns to sadness.

NOTES: *Line 5.* gorgias: derived from *gorge*, the gorgias were a starched linen or lace panel set in the front of a dress to cover the bosom and add decoration.
Line 9. getz: hair nets, similar to the snood.

Est breuis illa dies hodie : q̃ma forte dierum
Est michi sola dies : seu metuēdi dies

La mort
St vous aussi ge̅te bourgoise
pourueant certes vo⁹ euusez
il est force q̃ chim voise
Came voyez et aduisez
voz beaulx gorgias
empesez
Dy sont rien ne large
samoure
Maintz hommes en
sont abusez
En tous estatz il fault
mesure

La bourgoisse
es getz et colletz
de setisses
Ne me exemptent point
de mort
Mais mes grains ioye
et delices
Ne vieunet icy a remort
Ma cōscience fort me mort
de folies faictes en ieu
nesse
Qui me sont a rebour
tresfort
ioye en la fin tourne
en tristesse

Atque horrenda dies quia tunc meta merendi
Clauditur illa dies leta ve dira ve dies

La mort

1 Femme veufve venez avant
Et vous avancez de venir
Vous voyez les autres devant
Il convient une foiz finir
Cest belle chose de tenir
Lestat ou on est appellee
Et soy tousiours bien maintenir
8 Vertu est tout par tout louee

La femme veufve

9 Depuis que mon mary mourut
Jay eu affaire grandement
Sans ce que aucun me secourut
Si non de dieu gard seulement
Jay des enfans bien largement
Qui sont ieunes en non pourueux
Dont iay pitie mais nullement
16 Dieu ne laisse aucuns despourveux

A fearful day too, for then is the end of merit
Death chokes off that day, alas how fearful a day

Death

1 Widow, come forward.
Hurry yourself along.
You see the others ahead of you.
It's time to finish up, once and for all.
It's a fine thing to fill
The role to which you are called
And always to take good care of yourself.
8 Virtue is everything, everywhere praised.

The Widow

9 Ever since my husband died
I have had affairs to manage
Without help from anyone.
God's name alone protects.
I have many children,
Young, not provided for;
How I pity them,
16 But God leaves no one destitute.

Atq̄ horrenda dies: quia tunc meta metendi
Clauditur ista dies leta & dira de dies

La mort

Femme veufue
venez auant
Et vous auancez. &
xim̄r
vous vovez les autre
viuant
Il y aient vne foiz fin
Cest belle chose de tenir
En estat ou on est app
pelher
Et soy tousiours bien
maintenir
Vertu est tout par
tout louee

La femme veufue

Depuis que mon
mary mourut
Jay eu affaire grandem̄t
Sans ce que aucun
me secourut
Si no de dieu gard seule
ment
Jay des enfꝭ bn largem̄
Qui sont ieunes et nō
pourueux
Dont iay pitie mais
nullement
dieu ne laisse aucuns
esperacuy

Ortum suum quicumque repetunt terramque sequuntur
Flos fluit umbra fugit omnia nata cadunt

La mort

1 Alons oultre gente marchande
Et ne vous chaille de poiser
La marchandise qu'on demande
Cest simplesse dy plus muser
A lame deussez aviser
Le temps sen va heure apres heure
Et nest tel que de bien yser
8 Le merite et bienfait demeure

La marchande

9 Qui gardera mon ouvrouer
Tandis que ie suis amalaise
Mes gens ne feront que iouer
Les biens leur viennent a leur aise
A dieu ma balance et ma chaise
Ou iay euz les xx diligents
Pour plus cher vendre dont me poise
16 Avarice decoit les gens

Everyone returns to his stock and reverts to the ground
The flower fades, shadows take flight, all creation fails

Death

1 Let's go forward, gentle Merchant,
And don't bother to weigh
The merchandise they are asking for.
It's madness to think about that anymore.
You must think about your soul.
Time goes by, hour after hour,
And all we can do is to use it well.
8 Merit and good conduct last.

The Merchant

9 Who will watch my shop
While I'm in trouble?
My employees will only play.
The goods come to them easily.
Farewell my scale, farewell my chair,
Where I watched so diligently
To sell more dearly [which weighs on me now]
16 Avarice cheats people.

Nil reputo longum dubius quod terminus angit
                 Crastina forte dies est michi sola dies

     La mort

1 Apres madame la ballive
  Des quaquetz tenus en leglise
  Juge avez par raison vive
  Maintes gens a la vostre guise
  Je vous signifie main mise
  Pour pourveoir autre en voz lieu
  Car au iourduy serez demise
8 Point ne se fault iouer a dieu

     La ballive

9 Que femme se plaint de legier
  La coustume nest pas nouvelle
  Et sentremettre de iuger
  Des faitz d'aultruy et non pas delle
  Chascune se repute telle
  Que ce quelle fait est bien fait
  Quonques mal ne fut dit par elle
16 Il nest riens au monde parfait

30 VERSO   For the end hems in, untrustingly I hold nothing as lasting
Translation   Tomorrow may perhaps be my only day

     Death

1 Come along, Madame Bailiff.
  In chitter chatter, in the church,
  You judged, with your fertile imagination,
  Many people just as you wished.
  I give you notice, by this seizure,
  In order to invest another in your stead.
  For today you will be dismissed.
8 You must not trifle with God.

     The Bailiff's Lady

9 So, women complain easily—
  That isn't news!—
  And bustle around judging others
  And not themselves.
  Every woman believes that
  What she does is good
  And that she had never said anything bad.
16 There is nothing perfect in the world.

NOTES: The *baillive* has appropriated some of the functions of her husband to honor daily social interactions, as the vocabulary suggests. The Bailiff was similar to a magistrate. Here are his functions, as defined in a 1611 French-English dictionary: BAILLI: m. A Bailife (but of much more authoritie than ours) a Magistrat appointed within a Prouince, or precinct certaine, to execute iustice, maintaine the peace, and preserve the people from oppression, vexation, and wrong: To which end he takes notice of treasons committee, false money coyned; robberies, and murthers done; rebellions, or seditions raised; unlawfull, or populer assemblies made; Armes borne, or souldiours leuied, without warrant; Protections or Sanctuaries violated; Pardons, and Charters abused; Faires, markets, freedomes, and other priuileges usurped, or uniustly stood on: Hee makes proclamations in his own name; he calls the Ban, and Arriereban; leads those that be raised by it; and appoints th'ordinarie musters of his Prouince: hee determines Appeales from the sentences of Prouosts, and other inferior

Iudges, at Assises, whereof he is the principall Iudge; and is thereby held the most proper Iudge for Gentlemen, who have euer pretended that their causes must bee decided at Assises; and yet for all that, (and though hee may have a Lieutenant) he is but a Deputie, either unto the king, or unto some lord; euery one whereof (unto the Chastellain) hath, or may have, a Bailli within his territories (Randle Cotgrave, *A Dictionarie of the French and English Tongues*).

Line 5. main mise: seizure, a legal term.
Line 6. Pourveoir: to invest, a legal term.
Line 7. demise: dismissed, a legal term.

Sed superest meritis mercedem sumere dignam
Optima pro meritis et viciosa pati

1 Doulce fille et belle pucelle
Ne vous chaille ia de laisser
La misere de vie mortelle
Qui convient a chascun passer
Car qui vouldroit bien tout trasser
Il na seurte narrest en lieu
Fors son sauvement pourchasser
8 Virginite plaist bien a dieu

La pucelle
9 En ce siecle ieune ne vieulx
Ne sont pas en grant seurete
De larmes sont souvent les yeulx
Plains pour ennuy de pourete
Se on a ioyeusete
Il vient apres un douleur
Pour ung bien double adversite
16 Plaisir mondain finist en pleurs

It lies ahead to receive just desserts for deeds
To enjoy the best or endure the worst

1 Sweet child, beautiful Virgin,
Don't be unhappy to leave
The misery of mortal life
That everyone must yield.
Whoever would try to trace every detail
Has no security, no binding contract,
Except in seeking his own salvation
8 Virginity is very pleasing to God.

The Virgin
9 In this time, young and old
Are not very safe.
We often weep
For the burden of poverty.
If you have a little happiness,
It comes after a grief.
For one good thing, two misfortunes.
16 Earthly pleasure ends in tears.

Sed superest meritis mercedem sumere digna
Optima pro meritis et viciosa puti

onlee fille et
belle pucelle
lle vous chaulle ta de
laisser
La misere de vie mortelle
Sonient achun passe
Car qui vouldroit bien
tout laisser
Il na seurte navrest
en lieu
fors son saunement
pour chasser
Oragnite plaust
bien a dieu

La pucelle
In ce siecle renne
ne vieulx
ne sont pas en grant
seurtce
De larmes sont souuel
les yeulx
plante pour ennuy de
pourtse
Ce on a vne ioyeusete
Il vient apres vb doulel
pour vng bien double
aduersite
plasir mondain si
mst en pleure

Aspice iudicium hoc metuendum iudice tanto
Qui vocat et venit illa timenda dies

La mort

1 Ne direz vous rien de nouveau
Madame la theologienne
Du testament vieulx ou nouveau
Vous voiez comme ie vous maine
Et estes ia fort ancienne
Il fait bon cecy recongnoistre
Et a bien mourir mettre peine
8 Cest beaucoup que de soy congnoistre

La theologienne

9 Femme qui de clergie respond
Pour avoir bruit ou quon lescoute
Est des morues de petit pont
Qui ont grans yeulx et ne voient goute
Sage est qui rondement si boute
Et qui trop veult savoir est beugle
Le hault monter souvent cher couste
16 Chascun en son fait est aveugle

Espy this dire judgement by such a great judge
Who calls and comes on that fearsome day

Death

1 Won't you say anything new,
Madame Theologian,
About the Old or New Testament?
You see how I lead you away
And you are already very old.
It is good to recognize this
And to take the trouble to die well.
8 It is a great thing to know yourself.

The Theologian

9 A woman who speaks as a member of the clergy,
To have a following or to be listened to,
Is one of the codfish on the Petit Pont
Who have large eyes and see nothing.
Wise is the one who sails smoothly around,
And the one who wants to know too much is a noisy calf.
Rising high often costs dearly.
16 We are all blind in our own deeds.

NOTES: This role is hitherto unknown and unattested so early: neither a nun nor a lay religious, the Theologian is clearly associated with public preaching. The Petit Pont that connected the Latin Quarter to the Ile de la Cité was a favorite and customary spot for male preachers to practice. The Theologian does not wear distinctive clothing; her gown is dark blue tinged with gold, her head covering is very similar to that of the Widow Lady (29 verso), and her book is undistinguished by its covering or markings. Only the Abbess, Prioress, Hypocrite, Theologian, and one Old Woman (a former servant) carry books; of these, the Theologian's is the largest, with thick clasps.

Line 11. Although the Petit Pont was not the major food or fish-market section of the city, fish were sold all along the river.

Aspice iudicial hec metuendum iudice tanto
Qui locat et lenit illa tunendir dies

La mort   La theologienne
Ie direz vous rie   Lemme qui de
De nouueau   Clergie respond
Indis sa theologienne   pour auoir bruit ou
Du testament vieulx   quon lescoute
ou nouueau   Est domeues de petit por
Vous voies comme   Qui ont grande ratur
te vous mayne   et ne voient goutte
Et estes ta fort sauem   Sage est ej rondement si
Il fait bon cecy recon   boute
gnoistre   Et qui trop veult sau
Et a bien mourir   est beugle
mettre peine   Le hault monter sou
Cest beaucoup que de   uent cher couste
soy congnoistre   Chun en so fait e aueugle

Ergo time te instrue corrige mentem
Vive mori presto debita ferre para

La mort

1 Apres nouvelle marie
Qui avez mis vostre desir
A dancer et estre paree
Pour festes et nopces choisir
En dansant ie vous viens saisir
Au iourduy serez mise en terre
Mort ne vient iamais a plaisir
8 Joye sen va comme feu de ferre

La nouvelle marie

9 Las demy an encor na pas
Que commance a tenir mesnage
Parquoy si tost passer le pas
Ne my est pas doulceur mais rage
Javoye desir en mariage
De faire mons et merveilles
Mais la mort par trop fort me charge
16 Ung peu de vent abat grans fueilles

Therefore be in dread, prepare yourself, order your mind
Live prepared to die, be ready to bear just desserts

Death

1 Come along, Newlywed,
Who have set your heart
On dancing and being beautifully dressed
For parties and for choosing your wedding day.
Dancing, I come to grab you.
Today you will be put in the ground.
Death never comes at your pleasure.
8 Joy flees like fire on straw.

The Newlywed

9 Alas! Not even half a year ago
I began to keep house.
Why die so soon?
It is not sweetness I feel but fury.
I desired in my marriage
To perform the wonders of the world
But Death weighs too heavily on me.
16 A little wind brings down many leaves.

Ergo time te instrue corrige mentem
Que mori presto debita ferre prica

La mort

Apres nouuelle
mariee
Qui auez vng vit desir
A danser et estre priee
pour festes et noxes
choisir
En dansant te vous
viens saisir
Autourdhui serez mise
en terre
Mort ne vient iamais
a plaisir
Son sen va commencer
a feure

La nouuelle mariee

Ha deny an
encor na pas
Que commance a te
nir mesnage
parquoy si tost passer
le pas
Ne my est pas vulce
mais rage
Iauoye a siren mariage
e sé mons mecueille
Mais la mort par trop
fort me chatage
Ong vn se vent a
bit grans fueilles

Dum licet et spacium datur ista relinque
Pro patria celi: qua sine fine dies

La mort

1 Femme grosse prenez laisir
Dentendre a vous legierement
Car huy mourrez cest le plaisir
De dieu et son commandement
Allons pas a pas bellement
Et gettant vostre cueur es cieulx
Et layez paour aucunement
8 Dieu ne fait riens que pour le mieulx

La femme grosse

9 Jauray bien petit de deduyt
De mon premier enfentement
Se recommande a dieu le fruit
Et mon ame pareillement
Helas bien cuydoye autrement
Avoir grant ioye en ma gesine
Mais tout va bien piteusement
16 Fortune tost se change et fine

While it is permitted and space is given, leave your things
For the kingdom of heaven: to that end, end your days

Death

1 Pregnant Woman, relax!
Because today you will die.
Such is God's pleasure and command
Let's go, step by step, nicely,
Sending your heart to heaven.
Don't be afraid.
8 God does everything for the best.

The Pregnant Woman

9 I shall have very little happiness
From my first labor.
So I commend the fruit to God
Along with my soul.
Alas, I certainly thought otherwise,
That I carried great joy in my womb,
But everything turns out pitifully.
16 Fortune changes and ends things quickly.

Retia sunt anime facundia sensus honores
Quid certas ad opes: retia sunt anime

La mort

1 Sa damoiselle du bon temps
A tout voz anciens atours
Il est de vous en venir temps
Nature a en vous pris son cours
Vous ne pouez vivre tousiours
Je vois devant venez apres
Et ne faictes point longs seiours
8 Vieilles gens sont de la mort pres

La vieille damoiselle

9 Jay voirement mon temps passe
Et ayme mieulx ainsi mourir
Que revoir ce qui est passe
Et tant de miseres courir
Jay veu poures gens langourir
Et autres choses dont me tais
Enfans pour bien vivre et mourir
16 Il nest plus grant bien que de paix

Eloquence, emotions, and honors—snares for the soul
For what purpose possessions—snares for the soul

Death

1 Debutante from the good old days
With all your old-fashioned headdresses
It is time for you to come.
Nature has run its course in you.
You can't live forever.
I look ahead, come along,
And don't linger too long.
8 Old women are close to death.

The Old Debutante

9 I have surely overstayed my time
And would rather die
Than review the past
And go through so much misery.
I have seen poor people languish
And other things I keep to myself.
Children, to live and die well
16 There is no greater blessing than peace.

NOTES: This role is not found in A and G.

Although marriage is crucial for many women in the poem, the text also includes single women who stand on the periphery of marriage (the Old Debutante, the Prostitute) or wholly outside of it (the Abbess, the Prioress, the Franciscan, the Nun, and the Virgin). For others, marital status is either not mentioned or irrelevant.

Line 2. The spinster wears the old-fashioned hennin, in style fully twenty years before this poem. The artist has not only given her the physical body of an old woman, but also a very outdated dress.

Recta sunt amuie fecundia sensus honorez
O md certas adopes · recta sunt amuie

La mort
Sa damoiselle du
bon temps
A tout les auciens atos
Il est de bous en benir
temps
Nature a en bous pris
son coure
Bous ne pouez bure
tousiours
Je bous denat benez apres
Et ne faites point long
seiours
Dieilles gens sont dela
mort pres

La pieille damoiselle
Jay bourement mo
temps passe
Et ayme mieulx ainsi
mourir
Que reuoir ce que est passe
Et tant de miseie touir
Jay beu poures gens
languoureu
Et autres choses dont
me tais
Enfans pour bien bi
ure et mourir
Il nest plus grant bi
que de paix

33 VERSO   Preter amare deum tibi nil applaudat in orbe
            Omnia nam pereunt preter amare deum

                    La mort
              1 Femme de grant devocion
                 Cloez voz heures et matines
                 Et laissez contemplation
                 Car iamais nyres a matines
                 Se voz prieres sont bien dignes
                 Elle vous vauldront devant dieu
                 Rien ne vallent souspirs ne signes
              8 Bonne operation tient lieu

                    La cordeliere
              9 Je remercie le createur
                 A qui plaist de m'envoier querre
                 En louant le bon redempteur
                 Des bien que ma donne sur terre
                 Aux tentacons ay eu guerre
                 Qui est moult forte a demener
                 Dieu aide qui le veult requerre
             16 Servir dieu est vivre et regner

33 VERSO   Except for the love of God nothing is a credit to you on earth
Translation For all things pass on except for the love of God

                    Death
              1 Woman of great piety,
                 Finish your Hours and Matins
                 And give up contemplation,
                 For you will never go to Matins again.
                 If your prayers are worthy,
                 They will sustain you before God.
                 Sighs and crossing yourself are worth nothing.
              8 Good works replace them.

                    The Franciscan
              9 I thank the Creator
                 Who is pleased to seek me.
                 Praising the Good Redeemer
                 For the good things given me on earth;
                 I have fought temptation
                 Which is hard to resist.
                 God helps whoever seeks aid.
             16 To serve God is to live and reign.

NOTES: Although the Poor Clares were the sister order of the Franciscans, the preferred name for this role is derived from the common Middle French *cordelier* (Franciscan monk). The text's insistence on Matins (mentioned twice) and contemplation suggests that Franciscan nuns were still cloistered in the late fifteenth century.

Preter amair deu tibi mℏ applaudat in orbe
Omnia nam pereunt preter amaire drum

La mort

Femme de grant
deuocion
Closez voz heures et ma-
tines
Et laisses contēplacio
Car tamaire nirez a
matines
Se voz prieres sont
bien signes
Estes vous haultronte
xuant dieu
Rien ne ballent son
spirs ne signes
Bonne opera tuet lieu

La cordeliere

Ie remercié le
createur
A qui plaist de memoire
querre
En louant le bon redep-
teur
Des bñs q̄ ma donne
sur terre
Aur telacons ay enquere
Qui est moult forte a
xemener
Dieu aide qui se beust
requerre
Seruir dieu est uiure et
reigner

Quoniam non est in morte qui memor sit tui
In inferno autem quis confitebitur tibi

La mort

1 Femme dacueilz aimable
A festier gens a plante
Aquis avez amys de table
Pour parler de ioyeusete
Le temps nest tel qu'il a este
Rien ne vault icy vacabont
Parler qui nest que vanite
8 Ceulx qui ont le bruit ont le bont

La femme dacueil

9 Au iourduy parents et amys
Promettent et mons et merveilles
Mais quant voient quon est bas mis
Ilz baissent estos les oreilles
Et sont aussi sours comme feuilles
Que vent fait voler par couples
Et que vallent promesses telles
16 Vrays ne sont pas les amys doubles

For in death there is no one who is mindful of you
And in Sheol who will praise you

Death

1 Lovable, Friendly Woman,
You set about pleasing people.
You have made table friends
To talk of happy things.
Time is not what it was.
The idler is worth nothing.
Talk is only vanity.
8 Those who get the credit take the fall.

The Friendly Woman

9 Today, relatives and friends
Promise the wonders of the world
But when they see someone brought low
They plug up their ears
And are as deaf as the leaves
Which the wind blows away two by two.
What are such promises worth?
16 Aren't friends two-faced?

Quoniam non est in morte qui memor sit tui
in inferno autem quis confitebitur tibi

La mort
Femme sacueilz
amyable
A sesuer gens a plante
A quis auez amys de table
Pour parler se royen
sete
Le temps nest tel qsl
a este
Rien ne baust ier bn
cabont
Parler qui nest q̄
sante
Ceulx qui ont se bruit
ont se bont

La femme sacueilz
Au iourduy parés
et amys
Promettent et mone
et meruesses
Mais quant vorent
quon est bas me
silz bnssét estossés oresse
et st aussi sours cde feuisses
Que bent fait boser
par couples
et que vassent ymesses
tesses
Mays ne sont pas
ses amys dubses

34 VERSO   Periit ista dies nescitur origo secundi
           An labor an requies sit transit gloria mundi

La mort

1 Apres nourrice vostre beau filz
  Nonobstant son couatouer
  Et son beau bonnet a troys filz
  Vous ne le menerez plus iouer
  Deslogez vous sans delaier
  Car tous deux vous mourrez ensemble
  Vous ne pouez plus cy tarder
8 La mort prent tout quent bon luy semble

La nourrice

9 A cest dance fault aller
  Comme font les presbytres aux seyne
  Ie voulsisse bien reculer
  Mais ie me sens la boce an lame
  Entre les bras de mon alaine
  Cest enfant meurt despidimie
  Cest grant pitie de mort soudaine
16 Il nest qui ait heure ne de mie

34 VERSO   That day passes, the dawn of the second is unknown
Translation Whether there be labor or rest, the glory of the world passes

Death

1 Wetnurse, follow your fair child.
  Notwithstanding his coverlet
  And his fine bonnet in three ply knit;
  You won't take him to play any more.
  Move along without delay,
  For you both will die together.
  You can't stay here any more.
8 Death takes all when it seems right.

The Wetnurse

9 I must go to the dance
  As the priests go to Communion.
  I would like to hang back
  But I feel swelling under my clothing,
  Between my arms, when I breathe.
  This child is dying of plague.
  Sudden death is a great pity.
16 One may not have an hour or a half hour.

NOTES: The Wetnurse wears a white apron and a white cap, both of which could easily be laundered. The sleeves covering her forearms are close-fitting to allow her freedom of movement, and the illustrator has both revealed and emphasized the full breasts essential to her occupation.

Exeunt ista dies nesciter origo secundi
An labor an requies sit transit gloria mundi

La mort

Pres nourrice
voz beau filz
Non obstat se courtoue
Et son beau bonnet a
troys filz
vous ne le menerez
plus voier
Deslaiez vo̕ sne deliuer
Car tous deux vous
mourrez ensemble
vous ne poues plus
cy tarder
La mort prent tout
quant bon luy semble

La nourrice

ceste dance fault
aller
Comme sont les pères
aux serne
Ie voulsisse bien reculer
Mais ie me sens la bouce
en lame
Entre les bras de mon
asame
Cest enfant meurt de
spidunne
Cest grant pitie de mort
soudaine
Il nest qat heure ne de
mr̕

La mort

1 Pas ne vous oubliray derriere
Venez apres moy sa la main
Entendez plaisante bergiere
On marchande cy main a main
Aux champs nirez plus soir ne matin
Veiller brebis ne garder bestes
Riens ne sera de vous demain
8 Apres les veilles sont les festes

La bergiere

9 Je prens congie du franc gontter
Que ie regrette a merveilles
Plus naura chapeau desglantier
Car voicy piteuses nouvelles
A dieu bergiers et pasturelles
Et les beaux champs que dieu fist croistre
A dieu fleurs et roses vermeilles
16 Il fault tous obeyr au maistre

Death

1 I will not leave you behind.
Come along, take my hand,
Listen, pretty Shepherdess,
We walk along hand in hand.
You won't go to the fields any more, morning or evening,
To watch the sheep and care for your animals.
There will be nothing left of you tomorrow.
8 After the vigils come the holidays.

The Shepherdess

9 I say goodbye to the stout shepherd
Whom I regret leaving greatly.
He won't ever have another hawthorne cap,
For here is sad news.
Goodbye shepherds, goodbye shepherdesses,
Goodbye fair fields that God made grow,
Goodbye flowers, goodbye red roses.
16 We must all obey the Master.

NOTES: The Shepherdess wears the apron and fitted sleeves of the domestic or rural working woman, along with a purse attached to her belt in which she might carry food for the day and her needlework. Her dark hat of heavy material offers appropriate protection for the out-of-doors.

Her dog appears, to the modern dog lover, to be an ancestor of the Bedlington terrier: white, short-haired, with a distinctively shaped neck and head that resemble that of a lamb. This is the only animal to appear in any of the illuminations, although there are many insects, birds, and droll, animallike, fantastic creatures in the borders.

La mort

Et ne vous
oubliez pas derrie
Venez apres moy si la
main
Entendez plaisante
bergiere
On marchande cy ma
tin main
Aux champs mez plus
sour ne main
veiller brebis ne gar
der bestes
Lune ne sert de vous
demain
Apres les veilles sont
les festes

La bergiere

Ie prens congie
Qui fait a conter
Que ie regrette a
merueilles
Plus naura chapeau
desglantier
Car voicy piteuses nou
uelles
Adieu bergiers et pa
sturelles
Et les beaux champs q
dieu fist croistre
Adieu fleurs et roses
vermeilles
Il fault tous obeyr
au maistre

La mort

1 Apres pouve viele aux potences
  Qui ne vous pouez soustenir
  Cy bas navez pas voz plaisances
  Aussi vous en convient venir
  Lautre siecle est a advenir
  Ou pour vostre mal et misere
  Pouez a grans biens parvenir
8 Dieu recompense tout en gloire

La femme aux potences

9 De vieillesse ne voy mais goute
  Parquoy ne crains gueres la mort
  Dix ans ya que iay la goute
  Et maladie me griefue fort
  Mes amys ont le mie a tort
  Et nay vaillant deux blans contens
  Dieu seul est tout mon reconfort
16 Apres la pluye vient le beau temps

Death

1 Come along, poor old Woman on Crutches.
  You can't support yourself.
  You have no pleasures here on earth.
  So it's best for you to come.
  The other world is in the future
  When for your pain and misery
  You can attain great wealth.
8 God repays everyone in glory.

The Woman on Crutches

9 I see nothing good in old age,
  Therefore I'm not afraid of Death.
  For ten years I've had gout
  And I'm so troubled by illness.
  My friends aren't nice to me,
  And I'm not worth two silver coins.
  God alone is my complete comfort.
16 After the rain comes the fair weather.

NOTES: *Line 14*. blans: very small silver coins worth five to ten *deniers* each, or a few cents today. The major units of value in silver were the denier (penny), the *sol* (twelve deniers), and the *livre* or pound (20 sols or *sous*, as the plural of sol was more commonly written). There were also many other types of silver coins in circulation, such as the *double* (two deniers), the *gros* (equivalent to one sol), the *obole* (half a denier), as well as a system of gold coins.

La mort

Apres poure vie
Les aux potences
Qui ne vous pouez
soustenir
Cy bas nauez pas
voz plaisances
Aussi vous en couuient
venir
Lautre siecle est a
aduenir
Ou pour vostre mal
et misere
Pouez a grans bien
paruenir
Dieu recompense tout
en gloire

La femme aux potences

De vieillesse ne
voy mais goute
Parquoy ne crains
gueres la mort
Dix ans y a que jay
la goute
Et maladie me gri
efue fort
Mes amis ont sur mie
a tort
Et nay vaillant deux
blans contens
Dieu seul est tout mo
reconfort
Apres la pluye vient
le beau temps

Non ex difformitate corporis defedatur anima
Sed ex putredine animae defedatur corpus ait seneca

La mort

1 Sa poure femme de village
  Suivez mon train sans plus tarder
  Plus ne vendrez oeufz ne fourmage
  Alez vostre panier vuider
  Se vous avez bien sceu garder
  Pourete pacience et perte
  Vous en pourrez moult amender
8 Chascun trouuerra sa desserte

La femme de village

9 Je prens la mort vaille qui vaille
  Bien en gre et en pacience
  Frans archiers ont prins ma poullaille
  Et eu toute ma substance
  De poures gens nully nen pense
  Entre voisins na charite
  Chascun veult avoir grant chevance
16 Nul na cure de pourete

Not by deformity of the body does the soul take blight
But by the rot of the soul is the body deformed, says Seneca

Death

1 Poor Village Woman,
  Follow my procession without delay.
  You won't sell eggs or cheese any more.
  Go empty your basket.
  If you have endured
  Poverty, long suffering, and loss,
  You will be satisfied.
8 Each will find his just desserts.

The Village Woman

9 I take Death for what it's worth,
  Willingly and patiently.
  Free archers have taken my chickens
  And everything I had.
  Nobody thinks about the poor.
  There is no charity among neighbors.
  Everyone wants to be rich.
16 No one cares for poverty.

NOTES: The Village Woman's lines have often been quoted by historians to illustrate the attitudes of the long-suffering civilian French population, welcoming Death after being robbed and pillaged by both English and French armies through the Hundred Years War. She is the only woman in the manuscript to carry baskets: one full of chicks, the other of eggs.

Line 11. Frans archiers: These trained bowmen served on foot, and they were named "free" because they were exempt from certain taxes and fiscal duties. They were obliged to march, when called up, for a fixed, monthly salary.

Non er disformitate corporis defecit anim̄
Sed ex putredine aie defecit corp̄ aut senem

La mort
a noure femme
de village
Suiuez mon train fas
plus tarder
plus ne vendrez œuf
ne fourmage
Asez bze pouuez vuider
De vous auez bien sceu
garder
Pouvete priueë et perte
& vous en pouurez mout
amender
Chascun trouuera sa
desserte

La feme de village
e prens la mort
Uuille q̄ vuille
bien en gre et en paciece
frans archiers ont
prins ma pouillaille
Et en toute ma sub
stance
de poures gens mil ̄y
nen pence
Entre voisins na cha
rite
Chascun veult auoir
grant cheuance
Hul na cure de pourete

La mort

1 Et vous madame la gourree
Vendu avez maintz surpliz
Dont de largent estez fourree
Et en sont voz coffres remplis
Apres tous souhaitz acomplis
Comment tout laisser et bailler
Selon la robbe on fait le plis
8 A tel potaige tel cuillier

La vieille

9 A tout mon cas bien recongnoistre
Je nay vescu sans reprouche
Me suis affeuble de mon maistre
Comme fait coquin de sa pouche
Jay souvent mis ces vins en brouche
Et lay fait despendre en ma guise
Mais maintenant la mort maproche
16 Tant va ele pot a leau quil brise

Death

1 And you, Lady Languid,
Have sold lots of "surplus" items
And have provided for yourself from the money.
Your coffers are full.
After getting everything you wanted,
How to leave it all? How to hand it over?
According to the dress, the pleat is made.
8 For such a soup, such a spoon.

The Old Woman

9 I admit everything:
I haven't lived without reproach.
I clothed myself from my master
As a thief does, from his pocket.
I have often made hot wine from his cellar,
And I have made him spend the way I wanted.
Now Death comes near me.
16 If the pot goes to the well too often, it breaks.

NOTES: This woman appears only in B and C.

La mort

Et vous madie
la gourree
Vendu auez mainte
furpliz
Dont x largent este
fourree
Et en sont vos coffres
remplis
Apres tous souhaitz
a complis
Comment tout lais
ser et huiller
Selon la robbe on fau
se plie
A tel potaige tel cuil
lier

La vieille

Tout mon cas
bien recognoistre
Se nay lesen sans re
prouche
Ie x suis affeuble de
mon maistre
Comme fait chaiun
x sa pouesle
Iay souuent mis ces
vins en bouche
Et lay fait espendre
en ma guise
Mais maintenant
la mort ma pousche
Tant va le pot aleau
quil brise

La mort

1 Approuchez vous revenderesse
Sans plus cy faire demouree
Vostre corps nuyt et iour ne cesse
De gaigner pour estre honnoree
Honneur est de poure duree
Et se part en ung moment dheure
Au monde na chose assuree
8 Tel rit au matin qui au soir pleure

La revenderesse

9 Jauoye hier gaigne deux escus
Pour sourfaire subtillement
Mais ne scay qui les ma tollus
Argent acquis mauvaisement
Ne fait ia bien communement
Helas ie meurs cest dautre metz
Que prestre aye hastivement
16 Car il vault mieulx tart que iamais

Death

1 Come closer, Saleswoman,
Without waiting any longer.
You don't pause, night and day,
Earning to be respected.
Respect doesn't last long;
It is gone in one minute.
Nothing is certain in this world.
8 Who laughs in the morning cries at night.

The Saleswoman

9 Yesterday I had earned two ecus
Through clever overcharging,
But I don't know who took them from me.
Money gained dishonestly
Doesn't ever do any good.
Alas, I'm dying, that's another matter.
Let me have a priest quickly,
16 Better late than never.

NOTES: *Line 9*. escus: The *ecu* and *franc* were the primary units of gold coinage; one franc was worth approximately sixteen sous, and one ecu equalled three or four francs. Four manuscripts show instead *salus*, coins worth two and a half francs.

La mort

La reuenderesse

Approuche vo͂
reuenderesse
Sans plus ey faire
demouree
Vostre corps nupt et
iour ne cesse
De gaigner pour estre
honnoree
honneur est de poure
duree
Et se part en vng mo
ment sheure
Au monde na chose
asseuree
Tel rit au matin q͂
au soir pleure

Enuoie hier qui
que dent escus
Pour sourfaire sub
tillement
Mais ne scay qui
lez ma tollus
Argent acquis man
naisement
Ne fait ia bien com
munement
Helas ie meure cest
dittee metz
Que prestre aye hasti
uement
Car il vault mieulx
tart que iamais

La mort

1 Femme de petite value
Mal vivant en charnalite
Mene avez vie dissolue
En tout temps yver et este
Aiez le cueur espouente
Car vous serez de pres tenue
Pour mal faire on est tourmente
8 Peche nuist quant on continue

La femme amoureuse

9 A ce peche me suis soubzmise
Pour plaisance desordonee
Penduz soyent ceulx qui my ont mise
Et au mestier habandonnee
Las se ieusse este bien menee
Et conduite premierement
Iamais ny eusse este trouvee
16 La fin suit le commancement

Death

1 Worthless woman,
Living in carnal sin,
You have led a dissolute life
In every season, winter and summer.
Feel terror in your heart,
For you will be held tight.
One is tormented for doing bad things.
8 When one keeps doing it, sin is harmful.

Prostitute

9 I gave in to this sin
For unbridled pleasure.
Hang the ones who led me there
And left me to the trade.
If I had been well brought up
And guided in the first place,
I would never have been found like this.
16 The end follows the beginning.

La mort

Et ieunne et pente
   balue
A dix vinant en char
   nalite
Nene auec dit dif
   folue
En tout tempe vute
   et efte
Atez le cueur efpronte
Car vous ferez de
   pres temne
Pour malfaire on
   eft touvmente
Pefke miift quant
   on continue

La feme amoureuse

Ace pefke me
   fuis foubzmife
Pour plaifante de∫
   ordonnee
Pendus foyent ceulx
   qui mynt mife
Et au meftier habi
   donnee
Las fe reuffe efte bn
   menee
Et conduite pzeinie
   rement
Jamais ny euffe efte
   trouuee
La fin fut le comma
   cement

Noli per cras cras tibi longas ponere methas
Per cras cras cras cras omnis consumitur etas

La mort

1 Venez ca garde dacouchees
Dresse avez maintz baingz perdus
Et ces courtines atachees
Ou estoient beaulx boucquetz pendus
Biens y ont este despendus
Tant de motz ditz que cest ung ṣonge
Qui seront apres cher vendus
8 En la fin tout mal vient en ronge

La garde dacouchees

9 Iay voyrement dresse maintz baingz
Pour les comperes et commeres
Ou ont este patez de coingz
Mengez derioles goyeres
Tartes et fait mille grans cheres
Si tost quon a oste la table
Il nen souvient a nully gueres
16 Joye de menger est peu durable

---

38 RECTO
Translation

Do not lay out for yourself distant goals for the morrow, the morrow
For every age is spent tomorrow, tomorrow, tomorrow, tomorrow

Death

1 Come on, Bathhouse Attendant
You have drawn many wanted baths
And put up these bed curtains
Where beautiful bouquets were hung.
Lots of money has been spent,
So many words said that it's now a dream,
And they will be paid for dearly later.
8 In the end every bad deed gnaws at one's heart.

The Bathhouse Attendant

9 I have certainly arranged a lot of baths
For men and women;
Where quince pastries were eaten
And spicy cheese pies and tarts
And I have made a thousand big dinners.
As soon as the table is cleared
Scarcely anyone remembers it.
16 The joy of eating doesn't last.

NOTES: *Role name.* No dictionaries attest this compound term although both *garde* and *accouchee* are well-known forms meaning an attendant and a woman in childbed respectively. Here the activities described fit those of the bathhouse attendants, although why no version of the poem contains the assumedly conventional name *estuviere* for this role is a mystery.

Est homo res fragillis et durans tempore parue
Posset esse similis flori qui crescit in auro

La mort

1 Tirez vous pres gente garsette
Baille moy vostre bras menu
Il fault que sur vous la main mette
Vostre dernier iour est venu
Mort nesparge gros ne menu
Grant ou petit luy est tout ung
Paier on doit de tant tem
8 La mort est commune a chascun

La ieune fille

9 Ha a maniere ie suis happee
Vecy la morte qui me transporte
Pour dieu quon garde ma poupee
Mes cinq pierres ma belle cotte
Ou elle vient trestout emporte
Par le pouuoir que dieu luy donne
Vielz et ieunes de toute sort
16 Tout vient de dieu tout y retourne

Man is a fleeting being and lasts a short time
He should be likened to a flower that grows in the breeze

Death

1 Draw near, sweet little Girl,
Give me your tiny arm.
I must take hold of you;
Your last day has come.
Death doesn't spare fat or thin,
Big or small, it's all the same.
You have to pay, for so much time.
8 Death is common to everyone.

The Girl

9 Hey! Mother, I am caught.
Look, the dead woman is taking me away.
Please take care of my doll,
My five stones, my beautiful coat,
When Death comes, she takes away quickly,
By the power God gives her,
Old and young of every kind.
16 Everything comes from God; everything returns to Him.

NOTES: *Line 9.* Although F shows "a maniere" in the Girl's reply, three of the other four manuscripts have "ma mere" instead, hence "Mother" in the translation.

Est homo res fragillis et durans tempore paruo
Posset esse similis flori qui crescit in auro

La mort

Tirez vous pres
gente garsette
Baille moy vre bras
menu
il fault que sur vous
la main mette
Qze derner io est venu
Mort nesparge gros
ne menu
Grant ou petit tuy est
tout vng
payer on doit a tât ten
La mort est comu
ne a chascun

La ieune fille

Qu a maniere ie
suis happee
Dey la mort qui me
transporte
Si vien quon garde
ma poupee
Les cinq pierres ma
belle cotte
On este dict isto eporte
Par le pouuoir que
dieu suy somme
Prenez ieunes de toute
sorte Tout vient
de dieu tout y retorne

La mort

1 Suyuez mon train religieuse
De voz faitz convient rendre compte
Se point navez este piteuse
Aux poures ce vous sera honte
En paradis point on ne monte
Fors par degretz de charite
Entendez bien a vostre compte
8 Tout ce quon fait y est compte

La religieuse

9 Iay fait par tout ce que iay peu
Aux poures selon leur venue
Les malades pensez et repeu
Non si bien que iestoye tenue
Mais se faulte y est advenue
Dieu me pardonne la defaille
Sa grace tousiours retenue
16 Il nest si iuste qui ne faille

Death

1 Follow my procession, Sister,
You have to account for your deeds.
If you haven't shown pity
For the poor, you will be ashamed.
You don't rise to Paradise
Except by steps of charity.
Study your account.
8 Everything you do is counted there.

The Nun

9 Everywhere I have done what I could
For the poor, without discriminating.
I ministered to the sick and fed them
Not as well as people thought,
But if I have failed,
May God forgive my failure,
Always sustained by His Grace.
16 No one is so righteous he does not sin.

NOTES: The Nun wears the habit of the Dominicans, as does the Hypocrite (42 recto). She has been involved in caring for the poor and the sick, both common activities for nuns.

La mort

Suyuez mō trai
religieuse
De vo3 faitz connuient
rendre compte
De point naues este
piteuse
Aux poures ce vous
sera honte
En paradis point on
ne monte
Fors par degretz de
charite
Entendez bien a ve
compte
Tout ce quon fait y
est compte

La religieuse

Jay fait par tout
ce que ray peu
Aux poures selon leur
venue
Les malades pense3
et repeu
Non si bien q restoyr
tenue
Mais se faulte y est
aduenue
Dieu me pardonne
la defaulte
Sa grace tousiours
retenue
Il nest si iuste qui
ne faulte

La mort

1 Oyez oyez on vous fait assavoir
Tous que ceste vieille sorciere
A fait mourir et decepuoir
Plusieurs gens en mainte maniere
Est condemenee comme meurtriere
A mourir ne vivra plus gaire
Je la mayne en son cymitiere
8 Cest belle chose de bien faire

La sorciere

9 Mes bonnes gens ayez pitie
De moy las poure pecheresse
Et me donnez par amytie
Don de pastenostre ou de messe
Jay fait du mal en ma ieunesse
Dont icy achete la prune
Si priez dieu que mon ame adresse
16 Nul ne peult contre sa fortune

Death

1 Hear ye! Hear ye! Know ye all
That this old witch
Has caused the death and deception
Of several people in many ways.
She is condemned as a murderess
To die. She won't live much longer.
I'm taking her to her grave.
8 It's a fine thing to do good.

The Witch

9 My good people, have pity
On me, a poor sinner,
And give me, for mercy's sake,
The gift of an Our Father or a Mass.
I did wrong in my youth
For which I now pay the price.
Pray God redeem my soul.
16 No one can do anything contrary to one's destiny.

NOTES: The role of the Witch is not found in A or G.

Lines 1–8. Death uses the formal language of the court to make a public indictment. The Witch also addresses the public, begging mercy for her life of sin, which she attributes to errors of youth. Death calls her old.

The Witch is depicted as an unattractive woman in a baggy, undistinguished gown, with dishevelled hair, unbound and uncombed. She steps from the fireplace, traditional site of satanic rituals, and she holds a straw broom, either to ride or to feed the devil's goat.

Line 14. prune: literally, the plum.

La mort

rez oyez, on vous
fait assauoir
Tous que ceste vieille
soraciere
A fait mourir et de
ceuoir
Plusieurs gens en
mainte maniere
Est condēnee cōe
meurtriere
A mourir ne viura
plus gaire
Je la mayne en son
cymitiere
Cest belle chose de bien
faire

La soraciere

Es bonnes gens
ayez pitie
De moy las poure pe
cheresse
Et me soyiez par
amytie
Don de patenostre ou
de messe
Jay fait du mal en
ma ieunesse
Dont icy achete sa pu
ne
Si pries dieu que mon
ame adresse
Nul ne puest contre
sa fortune

Prout quicumque dies sibi longos estimat errat
Nulli est tota dies vivere tuta dies

La mort

1 Pour vous monstrer vostre folie
Et quon doit sur la mort veiller
Ca la main espousee iolye
Allons nous en deshabiller
Pour vous ne fault plus travailler
Car vous viendres coucher ailleurs
On ne se doit trop resveiller
8 Les faitz de dieu sont merveilleux

Lespousee

9 En la iournee quavoye desir
Davoir quelque ioye en ma vie
Ie nay que dueilz desplaisir
Et si fault que tantost devie
He mort pourquoy as tu envie
De moy qui me prens si acoup
Si grant faulte nay desservie
16 Mais il fault louer dieu de tout

Whoever reckons length of days for herself is amiss
To no one are all one's days secure

Death

1 To show you your folly
And to show that people ought to watch out for Death,
Take my hand, pretty Bride.
Let's go take off our clothes;
There's no more work for you
You will come to bed in another place.
You shouldn't get too excited.
8 God's acts are marvelous.

The Bride

9 On the very day I desired
To have a special joy in my life,
I only get grief, unhappiness,
And I must die so suddenly.
Death, why do you lust
For me, why take me so quickly?
I haven't deserved such a blow.
16 But we must praise God for everything.

NOTES: It is fitting that the Bride should be the most beautiful woman in the illuminations; the wedding day was the most significant day of a medieval woman's life.

The poet includes all of the formal stages of marital life in the poem—Debutante and Chambermaid in courtship, Bride, Newlywed, and Widow—along with six women whose status is derived exclusively from their husbands' roles (Queen, Duchess, Regent, Knight's Lady, Squire's Lady, and Bailiff's Lady). In all, over a third of the participants in the dance are identified in relation to marriage, clearly the focal point of medieval woman's identity.

Proth quicquid dies sibi longos estat erat
Iussi est tota dies vivit tuta dies

La mort

Pour vous monstrer
Vostre folie
Et quon soit sur la mort
veiller
Si la main espousee iolye
Allons nous en deshabiller
Pour vous ne fault
plus travailler
Car vous viendres con
cher ailleurs
On ne se doit trop res
veiller Les fautz de
dieu sont merveilleux

Lespousee

En la iournee
equanoxe desir
Amoir quelque ioye
en ma vie
Ie nay q ueil z desplaisir
Et si fault q tatost senue
He mort pourquoy
as tu envie
De moy qui me prens
si acoup
Si grant faulte nay
desservie
Mais il fault louer
dieu de tout

Frustra dico dies sit mentio nulla dierum
Cum stet nulla dies una nec hora quies

La mort

1 Femme nourrie en mignotise
Qui dormez iusques au disner
On va chauffer vostre chemise
Il est temps de vous desieuner
Vous ne deussiez iamaiz ieuner
Car vous estes trop maigre et vuide
A demain vous viens adiourner
8 On meurt plus tost que on ne cuide

La femme mignote

9 Pour dieu q'on me voise querir
Medicin ou appoticaire
Et comme me fault il mourir
Jay mary de si bon affaire
Anneaulx robes neuf ou dix paire
Ce morceau cy mest trop aigret
Moult se passe tost vaine gloire
16 Femme en ses faulx meurt a regret

40 VERSO
Translation

I consider the day vain, let there be no talk of days
When no day stands firm, no hour of rest

Death

1 Wife kept in the lap of luxury,
You sleep until dinner
Your chemise is being warmed
It is time to have your breakfast.
You should never fast,
For you are too thin and hollow.
I come to cancel your tomorrow.
8 People die sooner than they think.

The Darling Wife

9 For God's sake, go get
The doctor or apothecary.
Why must I die?
I have such a successful husband,
Rings, dresses, nine or ten pair.
This news is too harsh for me.
Vainglory goes away so soon.
16 A woman in sin dies with regret.

NOTES: This role, although recognizable to fifteenth-century readers, is without a specific, individualizing name, which forced the poet to invent one. *Mignote* means dainty, favorite, pampered, darling. She is shown rising from her large bed, still wearing her bedcap and a luxurious bedgown that falls open provocatively. The only woman to ask why she must die, she is also the only participant to cite her husband's successes and her own material possessions as reasons why she should live. She is accustomed to creature comforts. She is also a dieter, preoccupied with her slender figure, and is wealthy enough to have consulted both doctors and apothecaries.

Non est illa dies cursus ut ista dierum
Est deus illa dies ultima nostra quies

La mort

1
2 Renommee bonne chamberiere
Respondez au moins quant on huche
Sans tenir si rude maniere
Vous ne irez plus a la riviere
Baver au four ne ala fenestre
Cest cy vostre journee derniere
8 Aussi tost meurt servant que maistre

La chamberiere

9 Quoy ma maistresse ma promis
Me marier et des biens faire
Et puys si ay dautres amys
Qui luy aideront a parfaire
He men iray ie sans rien faire
Jen appelle on me fait tort
Aussi ne men sauroye taire
16 Peu de gens desirent la mort

That day is not a passage of days like this one
That last day, God, is our last rest.

Death

1
2 Maid of good reputation,
Answer when somebody calls you
Without acting so rude.
You won't go to the river again
Or gossip at oven or window.
This is your last day.
8 The servant dies as quickly as the master.

The Chambermaid

9 What! My mistress promised
To arrange my marriage and give me a dowry,
And besides I have other friends
Who will help her do it up right.
Oh! I will be leaving without doing anything.
I appeal, it's wrong.
I wouldn't know how to keep quiet.
16 Few people want Death.

NOTES: The Chambermaid, distaff tucked under her arm, wears a white apron, white fitted forearm sleeves, and has wound the material of her headdress into a kind of turban shape. It is the same style of headcovering worn by the Bathhouse Attendant (38 recto), but the *garde d'accouchees* is shown with the side cloth panels down, hanging free, and the Chambermaid has wound hers up, away from her neck.

La mort

1 Savez vous recommanderesse
  Point ung bon lieu pour me loger
  Jay bien mestier que on madresse
  Car nul ne me veult herberger
  Mais ien feray tant desloger
  Que on cognoistra mon enseigne
  Mourir fault pour vous abreger
8 Nul ne pert que autre ne gaigne

La recommanderesse

9 En la mort na point damitie
  Et si ne fait riens pour requeste
  Or argent priere pitie
  Pour neant on sen rompt la teste
  Qui y veult resister est beste
  La mort a nully ne complaist
  Et fault tous dancer a sa feste
16 Mourir convient quant a Dieu plaist

Death

1 Do you know, Hosteler,
  Any good place for me to stay?
  I need an address from someone
  Because nobody wants to take me in.
  But I will make so many move out
  That they will recognize my sign.
  You must die, your days are cut short.
8 Someone's loss is someone else's gain.

The Hosteler

9 Death has no mercy.
  And does nothing at your request.
  Gold, silver, prayer, pity,
  You break your head in vain.
  It's stupid to resist.
  Death accommodates no one.
  All of us must dance at Death's party.
16 We have to die when God pleases.

NOTES: *Role name. Recommanderesse* is usually defined in etymological dictionaries as a woman who placed servants and wetnurses. The *rue des Recommanderesses* was a well-known street on the Right Bank in Paris, near the Place de la Grève. The text here indicates a Hosteler, who found accommodations for travelers. The woodcut illustrating this figure in the 1491 incunable shows a woman consulting a list of lodgings.

La mort

auez vous re
commanderesse
point vng bon lieu
pour me loger
Jay bien mestier que
on madresse
Car nul ne me veult
herberger
Mais ien feray tant
desloger
Que on cognoistra
mon enseigne
Mourir fault po' vo'
abreger
Nul ne pert que autre
ne gaigne

La recommanderesse

En la mort na
point daintie
Et si ne fait riens pour
requeste
Dargent priere
pitie
Pour neant on sen
rompt la teste
Qui y veult resister
est beste
La mort a nully ne
complaist
Et fault tous dancer
a sa feste
Mourir conuient quat
a dieu plaist

Si quis sentiret quo tendit et unde veniret
Numquam gauderet sed omni tempore fleret

La mort

1 Dieu ayme bien femmes devotes
Qui ont leurs consciences nettes
Et hait sur toutes ces bigotes
Portans chaperons sans cornetes
Comment aucunes seurs coletes
Lesquelles par ypocrisie
En pechez secretz sont infectes
8 Devant dieu et sa compagnie

La bigote

9 Pour beate me suis monstree
Souvent meilleur que ie nestoye
Aucun effors bien desieunee
Faisant semblant que ie ieunoye
Et de ma bouche barbetore
Sans dire ne mot ne lire
Je prie a dieu quen bonne voye
16 Plaise ma poure ame mettre

Whoever knew where she was going and when she will have arrived
Would never be merry but would always be weeping

Death

1 God surely loves pious women
Who have clear consciences
And he hates hypocrites above all.
They wear hoods without veils
Like some nuns, in high collars.
Through hypocrisy they
Are depraved, in secret sins,
8 Before God and His company.

The Hypocrite

9 I wore the look of someone blessed,
Often better than I was.
Without any effort I ate heartily
Pretending to fast,
With trembling mouth,
Not saying or reading a word,
I pray to God that it may please Him
16 To send my soul on the right path.

NOTES: The Hypocrite is a new role added in the 1491 printed edition and does not occur elsewhere. We do not know who wrote these lines.

Role name. Bigote, feminine for *bigot.* Both terms are traditionally attributed to the oath "By God!" used by English soldiers during the Hundred Years War, but the word *bigot* existed as a Norman surname for more than two hundred years before that, first attested in writings from 1155. As the text indicates, the bigote is a religious hypocrite, not a bigot or prejudiced person.

Si quis sentiret quo tendit et vnde venniret
Numqz gauderet sed omni tempore fleret

La mort

Dieu ayme bien
femes deuotes
Qui ont leurs conscie
ces nettes
Et sur toutes ces
Bigotes.
Portans esperons
fans cornetes
Cõment aucunes feurs
coletes
Lesquelles yypocrisie
en peches secrez sõt isettes
Deuant dieu et sa cõ
pagnie

La Bigote

Pour verite me
suis monstree
Souuent meilleur q̃
ie nestoye
Aucuneffois bñ deguy
nee
Faisant semblant q̃
ie cuinoye
Et de ma bouche barletoye
Sãs dire ne mot ne sye
Ie prie a dieu quen
bonne voye
Plaise ma poure ame
mettre

La mort

1 Sur tost margot venez avant
Estes vous maintenant derriere
Vous deussez ia estre devant
Et dancer toute la premiere
Quel contenance quel maniere
Ou est vostre fille marote
Ne vault faire si maigre chere
8 Car cest vostre derniere note

La sotte

9 Entre vous coinctes et iolies
Femmes oyez que ie vous dis
Laisses a heure voz folies
Car vous mourrez sans contredis
Se iay ne mesfait ne mesdie
A ceulx qui demeurent pardon
Requiers et a dieu paradis
16 Demander ne puis plus beau don

Death

1 Come along, Margot, you especially!
You are last now,
You should be first
And dance in the front.
What a face! What a style!
Where is your Fool's bauble?
You must not give such a cold performance
8 For this is your last tune.

The Fool

9 Trim, pretty ladies,
Hear what I have to say to you.
Leave your foolishness now
Because you will certainly die.
Since I've done no wrong, I haven't lied,
I ask forgiveness from those who stay behind,
And I ask paradise from God.
16 I can't ask for a finer gift.

NOTES: Like the preceding role, this one occurs only in the 1491 incunable. We do not know who wrote these verses.

Line 1. Margot is the traditional stage name used by the sotte; the word also means magpie, a chattering bird. The female Fool acted in the *sottie*, a particular type of comedy characterized by great license, rapid patter, and acrobatic clowning. She and her male counterpart, the *sot*, wore caps with asses' ears, carried little staffs decorated with bells and topped by little carved heads, and they wore parti-colored costumes.

Line 6. Marotte, derived from the sotte's stage name *Margot*, is the traditional name for the Fool's bauble.

La mort
Sur tost margot
venez auant
Estes vous mainte
nant derriere
Vous deussez ta estre
auant
Et dancer toute la
premiere
Quel contenance que
maniere
Ou est vostre fille
marote
Ne vault faire si
maigre chiex
Car cest vostre derme
re note

La sotte
Entre vous comites
et iolies
femmes ory que ie
vous dis
Laisses a heure voz
folies
Car vous mourrez
sans contredis
De tay ne messait
ne messie
A ceulx qui demeurét
pardon
Requiers et a dieu pa
radis
demander ne puis
plus beau don

L'acteur

1 Vous seigneurs et vous aussi dames
Qui contemples ceste paincture
Plaise vous prier pour les ames
De ceulx qui sont en sepulture
De mort neschappe creature
Alez venez aprez mourez
Cest vie quun bien peu ne dure
8 Faictes bien vous le trouverez

9 Iadis furent comme vous estes
Qui ainsi dancent en facon telle
Alans parlans comme vous faictes
De gens mors il nest plus nouvelle
Ne il nenchault dune senelle
Aux hoirs ne amys des trespasses
15 Mais quilz aient argent et vaisselle

Authority

1 You, lords, and you too, ladies,
Who contemplate this painting,
Please pray for the souls
Of those who are in the grave.
Nothing created escapes Death.
Go, come, and then you will die.
This life lasts only a little while.
8 Do good and you will find it.

9 Before, they were as you are,
The ones who dance in such a way.
They went about their business, they spoke, as you do.
There's no more news about the dead.
It is not worth a fig
To the heirs or friends of the departed,
15 Unless they get silver and plate.

NOTES: This same poem appears after the postlogue, on 44 verso.
Line 13. senelle: literally, shoe sole.

Lacteur.   trouuerez.

Ous seigneurs et   Uldie furent coe
bos aussi dames.   bous estes.
Qui contemples ceste   Qui ainsi dancent en
paincture.   facon telle
Plaise bous prier po⁹   Alans parlans comme
ses ames.   bous faictes.
De ceulx qui sont en   De gens mors il nest
sepulture.   plus nouuelle.
De mort neschappe crea   Ne il nenchault dune
ture.   senelle.
A sez benez apres mou   Aux hoirs ne amys des
rez.   trespasses.
Ceste bie quun bien   Mais quilz aient ar
peu ne dure.   gent et baisselle.
faictes bien bous le

Aiez deulx pitie cest assez

1 Puis que ainsi est que la mort soit certaine
Plus que autre rien terrible et douloureuse
Et que chose ne peult estre incertaine
Puis que en est la vie horrible et angoisseuse
Et soit si briefve et partant perilleuse
Las nostre vie en ceste vallee miserable
Il mest aduis pour le plus conuenable
Que nous deuons du tout entierement
Mettre soubz pie ce mode decepuable
10 Pour bien mourir et vivre longuement

11 Delaisser doit toute ioye mondaine
Et mener vie humble et religieuse
Qui monter veult a la tressouveraine
Cite des cieulx qui tant est glorieuse
La contempler doit tous iours lame eureuse
Qui ayme dieu et hait oeuvre de dyable
Suyvre les bons estre a tous charitable
Soy confesser souuent deuotement
Et messe ouyr qui tant est proufittable
20 Pour bien mourir et vivre longuemement

21 Trop sabuse homme qui demaine
Orgueil en luy et vie ambicieuse
Quant il scet bien que la mort tout emmaine
Qui vient souuent soudaine et merueilleuse
Mais doit penser la passion piteuse
Du redempteur et la peine doubtable
Denfer dans fin qui est menarrable
Le iour hatif du divin iugement
Et se pechez comme sage et notable
30 Pour bien mourir et vivre longuement

31 Mortelle femme et ame raisonnable
Se apres mort ne veulx estre damnable
Tu dois le jour une fois seulement
Penser du moins ta fin abhominable
35 Pour bien mourir et vivre longuement

36 Cy finis presentie opusculi

Have pity on them, that's enough.

1 Since it is so that Death is certain,
More terrible and painful than any other thing,
And since this cannot be uncertain,
Since life is horrible and full of agony
And may be so brief and yet so perilous,
Alas, since our life in this valley is miserable,
It seems to me most suitable
That we must absolutely
Trample on this false world
10 To die well and to live long.

11 One must give up every earthly joy
And lead a humble, pious life
If he would wish to rise to the sovereign
City of Heaven which is so glorious.
The happy soul must contemplate it forever,
Who loves God and hates the devil's work.
Follow the virtuous, be charitable to all,
Go to confession often, piously,
And hear Mass which is of such benefit,
20 To die well and to live long.

21 He deceives himself who lives
A life of pride and ambition today
When he knows well that Death takes everything away
That often comes suddenly—marvelously.
But he must think on the pitiful passion
Of the redeemer and on the fearful pain
Of hell without end, which is to be remembered,
On the sudden day of divine judgment,
And on his sins, like the wise and worthy,
30 To die well and to live long.

31 Mortal woman and thoughtful soul,
If you do not wish to be damned after death,
You must today, if only once,
At least think of your hideous end
35 To die well and to live long.

36 Here finishes the present little work.

NOTES: None of the other manuscripts contains this ballade. D and E end with a different poem, addressed to a proud, arrogant, rich person.

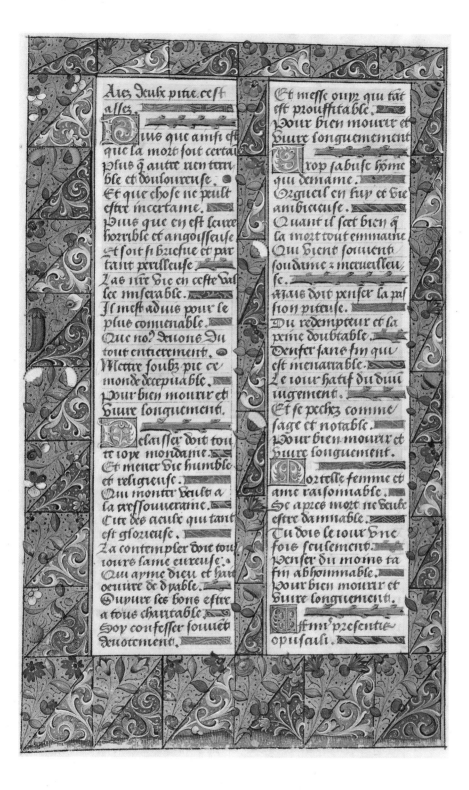

Aies deulx pitie ce st
asses.

Puis que ainsi est
que la mort soit certain
plus q̃ autre rien terri
ble et douloureuse.
Et que chose ne peult
estre incertaine.
Plus que en est seure
horrible et angoisseuse.
Et soit si briefue et par
tant perilleuse.
Las nre vie en ceste val
see miserable.
Il mest aduis pour le
plus conuenable.
Que nous deuons du
tout entierement.
Mettre soubz pie ce
monde deceptiable.
Pour bien mourir et
viure longuement.

Delaisser doit tou
te ioye mondaine.
Et mener vie humble
et religieuse.
Qui monter veult a
la tressouueraine.
Cite des cieulx qui tant
est glorieuse.
La contempler doit tou
iours lame eureuse.
Qui ayme dieu et hair
oeuure de diable.
Supuir ses bons estre
a tous charitable.
Soy confesser souuet
deuotement.

Et messe ouyr qui tat
est prouffitable.
Pour bien mourir et
viure longuement.

Trop sabuse home
qui demaine.
Orgueil en luy et vie
ambicieuse.
Quant il scet bien q̃
la mort tout emmaine.
Qui vient souuent
soudaine z merueilleu
se.
Mais doit penser la pas
sion piteuse.
Du redempteur et la
peine doubtable.
Penser sans fin qui
est meuarrable.
Le iour hatif du diui
iugement.
Et se pechez comme
sage et notable.
Pour bien mourir et
viure longuement.

Mortelle femme et
ame raisonnable.
Se apres mort ne veult
estre dannable.
Tu dois le iour vne
fois seulement.
Penser du moins ta
fin abhominable.
Pour bien mourir et
viure longuement.

Finit presentie
opusculi.

Vermibus hic donor et sic ostendere conor
Qualiter hic ponor ponitur omnis honor.
Ut placet in longu vite spem temporis auge.
Ex nichilo nichilum moy erit atque nichil.
Mille fuere viri millem milia mille.
Corpus humo putruit. nomine fama caret.

La royne morte

1 Iestoye royne couronnee
Plus que autre doubtee et craincte
Quis suis icy aux vers donnee
Apres que de mors fus attainte
Sur la terre ie suis contrainte
Destre couchee a la renuerse
Pour quoy est dure ma complainte
8 Bien charie droit qui ne verse

9 Prenez y qui me regardez
Exemple pour vostre prouffit
Et de mal faire vous gardez
Je nen dis plus il me souffit.
Si non. car celluy qui vous fit.
Quant il vouldra vous deffera.
Deffaiz esties quant vous refit
16 Qui bien fera bien trouuera

Here I am given to the worms and thus I try to show
that how I am disposed so is disposed all honor
If it pleases, increase the hope of a long lifetime
from nothing, nothing for me, and nothingness
There were a thousand men—and a thousand thousand
The body decays in the soil and the name falls from memory

The Dead Queen

1 I was the crowned Queen,
More than any other dreaded and feared,
Who now am given to the worms.
After I had been caught by Death
I was thrown down on the earth
To be laid out on my back:
Therefore my lament is harsh.
8 He plows straight who does not swerve.

9 You who look at me, take away
An example for your benefit
And keep yourselves from doing ill.
I say no more about it, I have had enough.
Indeed not. The one who made you
Will destroy you when he wishes.
You were destroyed when he made you.
16 Whoever does good will find good.

NOTES: The full sixteen lines from the Dead Queen are found only in D, E, and F.
Line 3. Quis: Latinism for *qui.*

Vermibus hic donor. et sic ostendere conor
Qualiter hic ponor. pomitur omnis honor.
Vt placet in longu Vite spem temporis auge.
Et p nichilo nichilum mox erit atqz nichil.
Aüsse fuere Viri milleni milia mille.
Corpus humo putruit. nomme fama caret.

La royne morte.
Estoye royne cou
ronnee.
Je sus que autre doub
tee et cramte.
O me sius icy auly Vers
donnee.
Apres que de mort fus
atamte.
Sur sa terre ie suis con
trainte.

Destre couchee a sa ren
uerse.
Pour quoy est dure ma
complainte.
Bien chaire droit qui
ne Verse.

Renez y qui me
regardez.
Exemplez pour Vre prouffit
Et de mal farre Vous gardez.

L'acteur

1 Vous seigneurs et vous aussi dames
Qui contemples ceste paincture
Plaise vous prier pour les ames
De ceulx qui sont en sepulture
De mort neschappe creature
Alez. Venez apres mourres
Cest vie quun bien peu ne dure
8 Faictes bien vous letrouuerez

9 Iadis furent comme vous estes
Qui ainsi dancent en facon telle
Allans parlans come vous faictes
De gens mors il nest plus nouuelle
Ne il nen chault dune senelle
Aux hoirs ne amis des trespasses
Mais quilz a ent argent et vaisselle
16 Ayez deulx pitie cest assez

Authority

1 You, lords, and you too, ladies,
Who contemplate this painting,
Please pray for the souls
Of those who are in the grave.
Nothing created escapes Death.
Go, come, and then you will die.
This life lasts only a little while.
8 Do good and you will find it.

9 Before, they were as you are,
The ones who dance in such a way.
They went about their business, they spoke, as you do.
There's no more news about the dead.
It is not worth a fig
To the heirs or friends of the departed,
Unless they get silver and plate.
16 Have pity on them, that's enough.

NOTES: The same speech from *Acteur* also occurs on 43 recto. In D and E it is placed immediately after the Dead Queen, which may account for its repetition here.

Two of the five manuscripts (BN 1186, Arsenal 3637) add one more stanza, as follows:

1 Explicit la dance mortelle
Que ung chascun appellera
Cest une dance bien nouvelle
Ce dieu ples elle pourfitera
Pour ce qui la regardera
De bon cueur y prengne exemplaire
Et dic ung ave maria
8 Pour celle qui cy la fait faire. Amen

1 Here ends the Dance of Death,
Which will call each and every one.

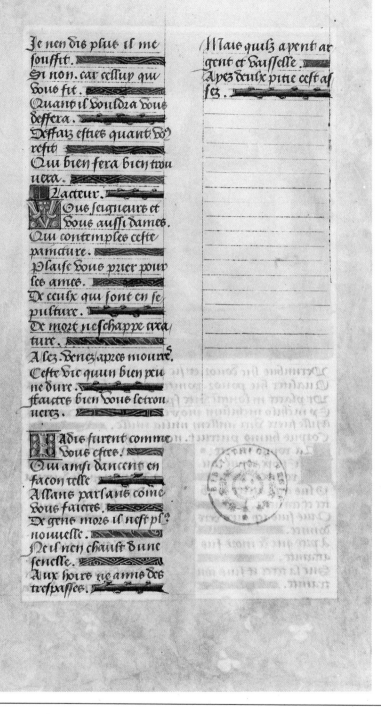

It is a very new dance.
Please God that it will benefit
The one who looks at it.
May this person take it to heart, as an example,
And say an Ave Maria
8 For the woman who is having it made. Amen

APPENDIX A

Variorum

Note: In this edition I have included only content variants, not orthographic or physical (arising from faulty manuscripts). Here is a sample of all variorum from four lines of folio 38 recto:

Line 1.

F	Venez ca garde dacouchees
A	Venez sa garde dacouchees
B	Venez ca garde dacouchees
C	Venez sa garde dacouchees
G	. . . es ca garde dacouciees

Line 2.

F	Dresse auez maintz baingz perdus
A	Qui avez drechie mainz baingz perdus
B	Ou auez dressez mains baings pdus
C	Qui auez dresses mains bains perduz
G	. . . essie auez mains bains perdus

Line 3.

F	Et ces cortines atachees
A	Et les courtines destachiees
B	Et les courtines attachees
C	Et les cortines destachees

Line 4.

F	Ou estoient beaulx boucquetz pendus
A	Ou sont les beaulx boucquetz pendus
B	Ou sont les biaulx bouquetz pendus
C	Ou sont les beaulx boucquetz penduz
G	. . . maint biens se sont despendus

From all of the variorum above, the following are content variants:

Line 3.   Et les courtines destachees (A, C)

Line 4. Ou sont les beaulx boucquetz panduz (A, B, C)
Line omitted (G).

There is only one content variant between F (B.N.fr. 995) and the printed editions (D and E). D and E show *la Morte* for *la Mort* throughout.

24 VERSO

1. Mires vous cy mires vous femmes (A)
    Myres vous ycy mirez dames (B)

9–16. Omitted (A, B, C, G)

25 RECTO

8. Vous qui vives ainsi serez (C, G)

25 VERSO

5. Il vous fault ennuyt trespasser (B, C)

13. Ja, des amys argent cheuance (A, B)
     Jay des amis argent finance (G)

15. Par quoy mest dure la sentence (A, B, G)

26 RECTO

2. Qui avez eu nom de si bien dire (A, C, G)

5. Vous soullies autres conduire (A)
    Vous souliez les autres conduire (B, C, G)

6. Festoiez gens e raliez (C)

11. Menestriels danceurs clarons (G)

12. Et des grands chiches que avons faites (G)

13. Mon cuer vit en ces entrefaictes (A)
     Mon ceur meurt entre ces entrefaictes (C)
     Mon cueur se meurt en ses contrefaites (G)
     Line omitted (B)

14. Mondanites nont cy plus lieu (A, B, C, G)

15. Mais tourmentez pouvres emplettes (A)
     Mais se tournent en poures amplettes (B)
     Mais tournent en pourez emplectes (C)
     Mais tournent en poures complaintes (G)

26 VERSO

3. Les engins vous fault habillier (A, B, G)

4.   Pour suivre le train de ma trasse (A, B, G)

16.   La fin de tous en dueil redonde (G)

1.   Dame plorez vos gorgerettes (B, C, G)

4.   Ne vous peuent de present aidier (B, C)
      Ne vous peuent maintenans aider (G)

7.   Chascunne y deust bien regarder (C)

14.   Au premier iour de may (A, B, C, G)

4.   Laissies fault dances et raguetz (A, C)
      Laissiez fault dances et ququetz (B)

5.   Vous venres en dautres banquetz (A, B, C)

6.   Ou les autres sentent laue roze (A)
      Ou les atours sentent eaue rose (B, C)

7.   Et verres jouster a Porquetz (A)
      Et verrez jouxtes aroquetz (B)
      Et verres iouxtes et rocquetz (C)

8.   Femme fait faire mainte chose (A, B, C)

10.   Mes habitz bobans et beaulte (A, B, C)

16.   Joye mondaine gueres ne dure (A, B, C)

7.   Maintes gens en sont abusez (A, B, C, G)

13.   Raison picque conscience mort (A, B, C, G)

14.   Et voy les folies de jeunesse (A, B, C, G)

15.   Qui sont a rebours cest au fort (A)
      Qui sont rebours desire fort (B, C, G)

16.   Jolivete tourne en tristesse (A, B, G)
      Joyeusete tourne en tristesse (C)

Role name: La vefue (C)
          La femme bossue (G)

1.   Femme veufve tirez avant (A, B, C)
      Femme bosue tires avant (G)

4.   Il convient une foiz finir (A, B, C, G)

5.   Lestat ou en bonne escarpellee (G)

10.   Des affaires ay eu grandement (A, B, C, G)

12.   Jay des enfans largement moulz (B)
      Jay des enfens moult largement (C, G)

15.   Dont jay pitie non pourtant (C)

30 RECTO

4.   Cest folie dy plus muser (A)
      Cest folie de tant muser (B, G)

8.   Le mercy et bien fait demeure (G)

15.   Et trop cher vendre dont me poise (A)
      Et de trop cher vendre me poise (B)
      Et trop cher vendu dont me poise (C)
      Et du trop chier vendu dont me poise (G)

30 VERSO

1.   Or sa madame la ballive (A, B, C, G)

3.   Qui avez juge par raison vive (A, B, C)

4.   Maintz vaillans gens a vostre guise (A, B, C, G)

5.   Pour pourveoir dautre en voz lieu (A, B, C, G)

9.   Femme si parle de legier (A, C)
      Femme si plaint de legier (B)
      Femme qui parle de legier (G)

10.   La coustume nest pas trop belle (G)

14.   Que ce quelle dit est bien fait (A, B, C, G)

15.   Mais on se brulle a la chandelle (A, B, C)
      Elle se brulle a la chandelle (G)

16.   Rien nya au monde parfait (C)
      Au monde ny a rien parfait (B, G)

31 RECTO

Role name: fille (B, C)
                pucelle vierge (E)

3.   La mesure de vie mortelle (G)

4.   Quil convient a chascun passer (A, G)
      Qui convient a chascun passer (B)
      Que convient a chascun passer (C)

5.   Qui vouldra bien tout trasser (C)
      Car qui veult bien par tout trasser (B)
      Car qui veut bien par tout penser (G)

6.   Il nya seurte narrest en lieu (A, C)
      Ny a seurete arrest ne lieu (G)

7.   Saulf son sauueur pourchassier (G)

10.   Ne sont pas a trop grant seurete (A, B, C)

11.   De pleurs et lermes sont les cieulx (A, B, C, G)

12.   Les meurs dennuy et pourete (A, B, C)
      Lon meurt denuy et pourete (G)

14.   Il vient apres quinze douleur (A, B, G)
      On a apres XV douleur (G)

31 VERSO

Role name: femme (B)
             scavante (G)

1.   Nous direz vous rien de nouveau (A, B)
     Vous dires vous rien de nouveau (C, G)

4.   Du fait du ciel et de larchanne (A, B)
     Des faiz du ciel et de la channe (C)
     Des fais de Dieu et de la vierge (G)

5.   Soubz vostre robe se gouverne (A, B, G)
     Soubz ugne robe se gouuerne (C)

6.   Ung sens acquis pare de maistre (A, B, C)
     Un sens acquis par art de maistre (G)

7.   Mais le drap si gaste la penne (A, B, C, G)

15.   Trop hault monter souvent chier couste (A, B, C)
     Trop haut monter souvent chiet dessus (G)

16.   Chacun est a son fait aveugle (G)

32 RECTO

1.   Apres nouvelle mariee (B, C, G)

4.   Pour dances et nopces choisir (C, G)

8.   Tout sen va comme feu de fuerre (G)

9.   Las demi an entier na pas (A, B, C, G)

10.   Que commencay tenir mesnage (B, C)
      Que commencay tout maisnage (G)

13.   Car javoie en mon courage (A)
      Can javoie bon petit courage (B, C, G)

14.   De dancer et faire merueilles (A)
      De marcher et faire merueilles (B, C)
      D'amacier faire merueilles (G)

16. Petit de vent abat grans fueilles (C, G)

32 VERSO

3. Ennuit mourrez cest le plaisir (B, C, G)

4. De dieu et par son mandement (A, B, C)

5. A tous pas a pas bellement (G)

6. En gettant vostre viz es cieulx (B)
   En getant nostre bras es cieulx (G)

9. Jauray bien petit du fruit (B)
   Iauray bien petit usuffruit (C)

33 RECTO

Role name: damoiselle (B)

1. Mademoiselle du bon temps (A, C, G)

4. Nature en vous a fait son cours (A, B, C, G)

5. Il nest joye viande ne amours (A, C)
   Joie nest viande namours (B)
   Il nest viande ne amours (G)

6. Qui vous puist exempter du trac (A, C)
   Que vous sceust exempter du trap (B)
   Qui vous examptent du tout (G)

7. On ne peut pas vivre tousiours (A, B, C, G)

8. Au bout de laune fault le drap (A, B, C, G)

11. Que revoir le vieulx temps passe (B, C)
    Que revoir le vieulx temps passer (G)

13. Pities poures gens langourir (A, B, C, G)

15. Et dautres choses dont me taiz (A, B, C, G)

33 VERSO

Role name: dame de religion (A)
              deuote (G)

2. Choyes vos heures et matines (C)
   Dones vos heures et matines (G)

3. En cessant contemplation (A, B, C, G)

6. Ilz serviront car dieu les ot (A, C)
   Elles servent car dieu les ot (B)
   Elles servent car Dieu les oit (G)

8. Tous fault mourir masches ce mot (A)
   Il fault mourir maschez ce mot (B, C)
   Il faut mourir tout ce quon voi (G)

11. En louant le vray redempteur (A)

13. Contre le monde ay eu la guerre (G)

14. Qui ma este forte a demener (B)
    Qui ma este fort a pourter (G)

15. Mais il ayde qui le veult requerre (A, B, C)
    Mais ie cuide qui le vont requerre (G)

34 RECTO

Role name: femme serette (A)
         femme (B, C)
         femme de chaire (G)

2. Pour faire soupe bien appreste (G)

3. Qui avez acquis amis de table (A, G)
   Qui avez quis amis en table (B)
   Qui avez acquis amys de taille (C)

5. Le temps nest plus tel qua este (A, C)
   Le temps nest tel qui a este (B)

6. Riens ny vault parler vacabond (A, B, C)
   Rien ny vaut parolle est morte (G)

7. Cest folie que de vanite (A, B, C)
   Cest folie que de conteste (G)

8. Ceux qui ont eu le bruit ont le bond (A, B, C)
   Contre celle qui tous emporte (G)

9. Jay eu des parentz et amis (A, B, C, G)

10. Qui mont promis mons et merueilles (A, B, C)
    Qui m'ont promis moult de merueilles (G)

12. Ils chaynent trestout les oreilles (A)
    Ils baissent trestous les oreilles (B, C, G)

15. Fiez vous en promesses telles (A, B, C, G)

16. Ces amis au jour dhuy sont doubles (A, B, C, G)

34 VERSO

1. Vous nourrice et vostre beau filz (A, B, C, G)

2. Nonobstant vostre couvrechaier (G)

3. Et son grant bonnet atrois filz (B, C)
   Et vostre grant bonnet a trois fils (G)

4-5. lines permuted (A, B, C, G)

7. Femmes vecy beau mirouer (A, B, C)
   Certes vecy beau mirouer (G)

8. Dieu prend seulx que bon lui samble (A)
La mort prent ceulx quant bon lui samble (B)
La mort prent ceulx qui bon luy semble (C)
La mort prent ceulx que bon luy semble (G)

10. Comme font les prebstres au same (A)
Comme font les prebstres au senne (B)
Comme font les prebstres au ceyne (C)
Comme font les prebstres au sen (G)

16. Nully na heure ne demie (B, C, G)

3 5 RECTO

1. Pas ne vous oubliray de rien (G)

3. Entendez vous plaisant bergere (A, B, C)
Entendes vous plaisant gorgette (G)

7. Il nest qui ait point de demain (A)
Personne nest qui ait demain (B)
Il ny a nul qui ayt demain (C)
Il nest personne qui ait demain (G)

10. A qui jay regret a merueilles (A, B, C, G)

11. Plus naray chapeau desglantier (A, B, C, G)

13. Adieu bergieres et pastourelles (A, B, G)
Adieu pastours et pastourelles (G)

16. Plus ne vous virray ja croistre (G)

3 5 VERSO

Role name: vielle (A, B, C)
vielle aus deux potences (G)

3. Cy bas navez eu voz plaisances (C, G)

5. Il n'a autre siecle avenir (B)
Il y a autre siecle advenir (C)
. . . y a autre siecle advenir (G)

7. Pouves a grant joie parvenier (A)
Pourrez a grant joie pervenir (B, C, G)

11. Il y a dix ans que jay la goutte (B, C)
. . . y a dix ans que iay la goute (G)

14. Et nay vaillant dix blans cantens (A)

15. Mais en dieu ay mon resconfort (A)
Mais en dieu est mon reconfort (B, C, G)

3 6 RECTO

Role name: villageoise (G)

12. Et oste toute ma substance (A, B, C)
   . . . toute ouster ma substance (G)

14. . . . ntre voisines na charite (G)

2. Qui avez venduz maintz surplis (C)

4. Et avez voz   remplis (B)
   Et avez voz choux rempliz (C)

6. Convient tout lais ser et bailler (C)

7. Selon la robe sont les plis (B, C)

11. De moy cest affable de mon maistre (B)
   De moy cest assote de mon maistre (C)

12. Comme ung coquin est de sa preche (B)
   Comme est ung coquin de sa pouche (C)

13. Par quoy jay mis ses vins en broche (B, C)

14. Le sien fait menger a sa guise (B, C)

15. Mais maintenant la mort saproche (B, C)

16. Tant va le pot a leau qui brise (C)

Role name: marchande (G)

3. Vostre cuer nuit et jour ne cesse (B, C, G)

6. Et se pert en mouvement deure (B)

9. Hier iauoie gagnie deux salus (A, B, C, G)

15. Que jaie le prebstre hastivement (B, C)
   Queres le prestre hastivement (G)

16. Il vault mieulx plus tart que james (A, C)
   Il vault mieux tart que james (B)

Role name: femme (B)
            femme commune (C)
            dissolue (G)

3. Qui mene auez vie dissolue (A)
   Qui avez menee vie dissolue (B)
   Qui avez mene vie dissolue (C)

10. Par plaisance desordonnee (A, B, C)
   Par plaisirs desordonnee (G)

11. Mauldis soient ceulx qui my ont mise (A, B, C, G) .

15.   Jamais ny eusse este tournee (A, B, C)

16.   La fin fait le commencement (G)

38 RECTO

2.   Qui avez drechie maintz baingz perdus (A, B, C, G)

3.   Et les courtines destachiees (A, B, C)

4.   Ou sont les beaulx boucquetz pendus (A, B, C)
    line omitted (G)

6.   Et tant de metz que cest un songe (B, C)
    . . . ant de maulx que cest un songe (G)

7.   Mais ilz sont apres chiers venduz (B, C)
    . . . ais ils sont a prou chier vendus (G)

11.   Veu drecer pastes de coings (A)
    Veu menger biaux pastez de coings (B, C)
    Beaux mengiers beaux pastes de coings (G)

12.   Tartes dariolles goyeres (A, B, C, G)

13.   Et faire cent milles grans cheres (A, B, C, G)

38 VERSO

5.   Je nespargne gros ne menu (A, B, C, G)

6.   Grant ou petit ce mest tout ung (A, B, C, G)

7.   Et prens tant paye tant tem (A, B, C, G)

9.   Ha ma mere je suis happee (B, C, G)

12.   Mon beau colet ma belle cote (G)

13.   Ou la mort vient trestout emporte (B)
    Car la mort vient qui tout convoite (G)

15.   Jongleurs danceurs de toute sorte (G)

39 RECTO

Role name: nonain (A)

2.   De vos fais venes rendre compte (G)

9.   Iay fait tout du mieulx que jai peu (A, B, C, G)

39 VERSO

6.   A mourir en feu et misere (B, C)

10.   De moy et de toute pecheresse (B, C)

11.   Et nous donnez par amitie (B)

15. Si priez dieu qui lame dresse (B, C)

1. Pour monstrer vanite folie (A, B, C, G)

7. On ne se doit trop recailler (B, C)
   Lon ne se doit trop reculer (G)

10. Dauoir quelque bien en ma vie (B)
    Dauoir moult de biens en ma vie (G)

Role name: financiere (G)

6. Car vous este trop maigre et unie (G)

9. Pour dieu que lon maille (B)
   He pour dieu con me vase guerre (G)

10. Medecin et appotiquaire (B, C)

12. Qui a mary de si bon affaire (B, C, G)

13. Annaux robes huit ou du paire (B)
    Aneaulx rubis neuf ou dix paire (C)
    Aneaus robes huit ou dix paire (G)

15. Et se passe tout vaine gloire (C)
    Et si passe toute bonne . . . (G)

1. Omitted in B.N.fr. 995
   Dictes jeune femme a la cruche (A, B, C)
   Entres jeune femme a la cruche (G)

4. Sans faire tant la sourde oreille (G)

6. Laver nau four na la fenestre (G)

7. Vecy vostre iournee derniere (A, G)
   Veez vostre iournee derniere (B, C)

12. Qui lui dovont et de quoy boire (G)

13. He morayie; en telle misere (G)

14. L'en appelle on me fait tort (G)

15. Et dautre part ne men puis taire (A)
    Et quant a moy ne men puys taire (B, C, G)

16. Pou de gens se loent de la mort (A, B, C, G)

1. O vous seigneurs et mes dames (A, B)
   A vous seigneurs et mes dames (C)
   (G does not contain this strophe.)

9. Jadis feusmes comme vous estes (A, B, C)

10. Vivans mengans en fasson telle (A, B, C)

11. Ne plus ne moins comme vous faictes (A)
    Ne plus ne moins comme vous estes (B, C)

12. Mais des gens mors nest plus nouuelle (A, B, C)

13. Ne nen chault pas dune cinelle (B)
    Nil nenchault dune cyuelle (C)

16. A, B, C, contain final line, omitted in F.
    Ayes en pittie cest assez.
    Translation: Have pity, that's enough.

Description of B.N.fr. 995 and Its Provenance

TEXT

A compendium of texts on death, including (1) *La Danse Macabre*, fols. 1–17, incipit "O Creature raisonnable/Qui desires vie eternelle," and explicit "Et faictes des biens, plus n'en dis/Bien fait vault moult aux trespasses"; (2) *Des Trois morts et des trois vifs*, fols. 17v–23, incipit "Euvre tes yeulx, creature chetive,/Vien veoir les fais de la mort excessive," and explicit "Le mal dancant aura pour satisfaire/Feu eternel puant, abhominable"; and (3) *La Danse Macabre des Femmes*, fols. 23v–44, incipit "Ludite formose, teneres cantate puelle . . . /Venez, dames et damoiselles," and explicit "Mais qui'ilz ayent argent et vaissalle/Ayez d'eulx pitie, c'est assez." The collation, in addition to the consistent illumination, indicates that the compendium was composed at one time and that the three texts were intended to go together.

ILLUSTRATIONS
Subjects of the Miniatures

La Danse Macabre

f. 1:	Author
f. 1v:	Death and the Pope
f. 2:	Death and the Emperor
f. 2v:	Death and the Cardinal
f. 3:	Death and the King
f. 4:	Death and the Constable
f. 4v:	Death and the Archbishop
f. 5:	Death and the Baron
f. 5v:	Death and the Bishop
f. 6:	Death and the Squire
f. 6v:	Death and the Abbot
f. 7:	Death and the Bailiff
f. 7v:	Death and the Schoolmaster
f. 8:	Death and the Bourgeois
f. 8v:	Death and the Canon

Les Trois morts

Borders

Four types of borders appear in the manuscript, as follows, from the simplest to the most complex:

Type I: pale pink and white acanthus leaves decorate a gold background, on which appear black pen flecks; other decoration includes pinecones, strawberries, flowers, and naked putti. Sometimes a green grassy mound decorates the bottom of the page, *i.e.,* fols. 1, 2, 3, 4, 17v, not used in the *Danse Macabre des Femmes.*

Type II: pink, blue, yellow, and orange acanthus leaves decorate a gold background, on which appear black pen flecks; other decoration includes putti along with other grotesques, such as skulls. Sometimes a green grassy mound decorates the bottom of the page, *i.e.,* fols. 1v, 2v, 4, 6, 6v, 7, etc., and occasionally in the *Danse Macabre des Femmes* on fols. 28, 29, 32.

Type III: evolves out of Type II and consists of a geometric pattern of which there are many variations, such as hearts (fol. 14), quatrefoils (fol. 12v), trefoils (fol. 3v), cinquefoils (fol. 19). Used frequently in the *Danse Macabre des Femmes* on fols. 24v, 25v, 26v, 27v, 28v, etc.

Type IV: illusionistic, more elaborate border of pink, lavender, green, blue, and red acanthus on a gold ground, on which the flowers, the animals, and the leaves cast shadows. Along with Type III, used frequently in the *Danse Macabre des Femmes* on fols. 24, 25, 26, 27, etc.

44 folios, on parchment, plus 8 contemporary parchment flyleaves, 4 in front and 4 in back, composed mostly of gatherings of eight, i⁴ (1–8), ii⁴ (9–16), iii⁴ (17–24), iv⁴ (25–32), v⁴ (33–40), vi² (41–44), modern foliation in ink, written in dark brown ink in a gothic *bâtarde* book-hand, in double columns, on 39–41 lines, ruled in red, rubrics in blue, line endings throughout in burnished gold on reddish-brown and blue grounds, 2–4 line foliate initials throughout in blue and pink acanthus on gold grounds, full illuminated borders on every page, except fol. 44v, including panel border between the 2 columns of script, of 4 designs of colored acanthus on gold grounds, 78 half-page miniatures, 130×120 to 133×122 mm., overall dimensions, 313×200 mm., justification, 272×168 to 277×168 mm.

BINDING

Seventeenth-century binding of red morocco gilt with the stamp (*D'Or à la couleuvre en pal tortillée d'azur*) of Jean-Baptiste Colbert, marquis de Seignelay; cf. Joannis Guigard, *Nouvel armorial du bibliophile. Guide de l'amateur des livres armoriés*, 2 vols. (Paris: Emile Rondeau, 1890).

PROVENANCE

1. an unidentified member of the de Rochefort Bruille family, who signed the first lower parchment flyleaf in the upper margin in a late sixteenth- (?) or seventeenth-century hand: *de Rochefort/Bruille*.
2. Jean-Baptiste Colbert, marquis de Seignelay (1619–1683), whose shelf mark appears on fol. 1 in the upper margin: *Colbert 1849*.
3. acquired in 1732 by the Bibliothèque Nationale along with Colbert's library; shelf mark on fol. 1 in the upper margin: *Regnus 7310*.

Catalogue Description
of Other Manuscripts

BIBLIOTHÈQUE NATIONALE, MS. FR.
1186.

1. "L'Espittre que Othea la deesse envoia à Hector de Troyes,
   quant'il estoit en l'eage de XV ans"
2. "La Dance aux aveugles [par GUILLAUME] Michault,"
   commençant (Fol. 55) par:
   "Attaint au cuer par ung couroulx terrestre,
   "Ou point secret d'une nuit nette et cler . . ."
   et finissant par:
   "Il leur plaise corrigier bas et hault
   "Leur escollier et disciple Michault."
3. Danse Macabre (Fol. 89)
   Papier, desseins coloriés 1482 (Anc. 7400)

BIBLIOTHÈQUE NATIONALE, MS. FR.
10032. RECUEIL D'ANCIENNES POÉSIES
FRANÇAISES.

Fol. 2. "Le Mirouer du pecheur, translaté par Castel, croniqueur de
Franche." —Fol. 27. "Livre du lax d'amour, contemplacion pour l'ame
devote sur la Passion." —Fol. 65 v°. Dialogue, en vers, entre Marie,
l'âme, l'hôtesse et Jésus-Christ. —Fol. 87. "Belle meditacion pour penser à la mort." —Fol. 99. "Manuel saint Augustin." —Fol. 123. "Jardin
esperituel pour religieux et religieuses." —Fol. 131 v°. "Miroir des
dames et des demoiselles." —Fol. 135. "Balade pour avoir paix a Dieu
et au monde," et autres balades et rondeaux. —Fol. 157. "Le Miroir
du monde," et autres poésies morales. —Fol. 171. "La revelacion de
Theophile et de ce qu'il trouva en enfer," etc. —Fol. 180 v°. "Les VII.
Psaulmes, en franchois." —Fol. 193. "Le debat de l'omme mondain et
de son compaignon qui se veult rendre religieux." —Fol. 206 v°.
"L'enseignement . . . de S. Pierre l'appostre à Simon le corier." —Fol.
209. "La danse machabrée." —Fol. 224. "La dance des femmes, composée à Paris." —Fol. 238 v°. "La bataille des vices et vertus." —Fol.

241. "Devote instruction comment on doit porter le croix de Jhesu-crist..." —Fol. 243. "Le Miroir du monde." —Fol. 251. "Le debat de l'omme et de la femme" et "Rondeau de Nostre Dame," par Guillaume Alexis, prieur de Bucy. —Fol. 259. "Traictié par forme de quolibetz pour respondre à touz propos" [Faintes du monde, par Guillaume Alexis].

XVe siècle. Papier. 280 feuillets. 130 sur 90 millim. Relieure maroquin grenat. (N° 340 de la collection Barrois.)

BIBLIOTHÈQUE NATIONALE, MS. FR. 25434. DANCE MACABRÉ, ET AUTRES POESIES DE MARTIAL D'AUVERGNE, GEORGES CHASTELLAIN, CHRISTINE DE PISAN, ALAIN CHARTIER ET PIERRE D'AILLY.

Fol. 1.	"Le Débat de l'homme mondain et de son compaignon qui veult estre religieux."
	"Mon compaignon, que veulx tu faire
	De te rendre religieux..."
Fol. 18.	"La Dance Machabré des hommes."
	"L'acteur, O creature raysonnable,
	Qui desires vie eternelle..."
Fol. 36.	"Dit de la mort, composé par ung Celestin."
	"La mort. Se mon regard ne vous vient a plaisir
	Pour sa hydeur, qui est espoventable..."
Fol. 41.	"Le Breviaire des nobles, composé par maistre Alain Chartier."
	"Le noblesse, dame de bon vouloir,
	Royne des preux, princesse des haulx faiz..."
Fol. 55 v°.	"Dictamen de beata Maria Virgine."
	"Altitonantis apex ancillam aspexit ab alto..."
Fol. 57 v°.	"Duodecim paladini Francie;" "Turcus as papam, etc.
Fol. 58.	"Les Enfermetéz du corps," par Pierre d'Ailly; cf. Romania, t. XXIX, p. 114.
Fol. 60.	"Beau dictié."
	"Li aujourdhui veulx vivre en paix..."
Fol. 61.	"La Dance des femmes, la quelle composa maistre Marcial d'Auvergne."
	"L'acteur. Mirez vous icy, mirez femmes,
	Pour prendre consolation..."
Fol. 80 v°.	Piteuse complainte de George Chastellain aux puissances célestes de la vie humaine, et autres ballades de lui.
	"Dieu glorieux, angelz, sainz et saintines,
	Celestines puissances supernelles..."
Fol. 99 v°.	"Les dix Commandemens de la loy."
	"Ung seul Dieu, de tout createur,
	Tu serviras et aymeras..."

Fol. 101.   "Facet, en françoys.
                 "Chaton, qui fun ung saige homs,
                 De qui l'enseignement avons..."
Fol. 116 v°.   "Cy ensuyt Christine de Pise, auquel y a plusieurs
                 bons enseignemens touchant le monde."
                 "Filz, je n'ay mye grans tresors
                 A t'enrichir, pour ce tresor..."
Fol. 132.   "Torneamentum monachorum."
                 "Quando nocte video in choro conventum,
                 Ad laudem dominicam quemlibet intentum..."
Fol. 134 v°.   Règle de vie, en vers.
                 "Humble maintien, joyeux et asseure,
                 Langage meur, amoureux, veritable..."
Fol. 137.   "Cinq choses causantes la peste, commençant par F.,
                 c'est assavoir: Fain, Fruictz, Femme, Frayeur et Front."

XVe siecle. Papier. 137 feuillets. 135 sur 95 millimètres. Rel. peau verte. (Celestins 47.)

A R S É N A L   3 6 3 7   (2 9 6   B .   F .)
P O É S I E S   D E   D E N I S   C A T I N ,   C U R É   D E
M E U D O N .

1. —Fol. 1. "Un petit traictié appellé les Contredictz du regulier et seculier, Fait par Me Denis Catin, en karesme cinq cens dix-et-huit."
    —Prologue:
        "Tout triste, ung de ces jours passés,
        Mil pensées se funderent en moy..."
    Commencement:
        "Ceur amorti, plorable, parti, accusatif,
        Tout circuy de mondain vitupayre..."
L'explicit est de la main de l'auteur, avec signature autographe.
2. —Fol. 26. "Fragment rhimé d'une dance feminine, dicte machabre, compozée par Mr. Denis Catin, docteur en doirt canon et curé de Meudon, l'an Domini 1519."
    Commencement: LA DUCHESSE
        "Je n'ay pas encores XXX ans.
        Hélàs, à l'eure que je commance
        Assavoir que c'est du bon temps,
        La mort vient tollir ma plaisance..."

Papier. 30 feuillets. 170 sur 130 millim. Ecriture du XVIe siècle, à longues lignes aux Fol. 1-25; sur 2 col. aux Fol. 26-30.

De la bibliothèque de M. de Paulmy, "Belles-Lettres, no. 1563" et "1817".

Couvert en parchemin blanc.

BIBLIOTHÈQUE NATIONALE 4105.
DANSE MACABRÉE; DIT DES TROIS
MORTS ET DES TROIS VIFS. —DANSE
MACABRÉE DES FEMMES; DÉBAT DU
CORPS ET DE L'ÂME; COMPLAINTE DE
L'ÂME DAMNÉE. —PARISIIS, GUIDO
MARCHANT, 1486, 7 JUNII–7 JULII.

33 ffnc.; car. goth. 2 grand., type 2 (gros car. Thierry-Poux VIII, 2,
3 et Claudin I, p. 336, alph., et p. 337 au haut) type 4 (pet. car.
Claudin p. 401, 2e alph.); 2 col. ou ll. ll. de nombre variable; signat.
a–d, par 8 ff; init. grav.; gravures (Claudin I, pp. 338–350, 352 et
360. Monceaux, *Les Le Rouge* I pp. 136 et 137, réduites); pet. in-fol.
B. Nat. Ye 189, exposé 270.

BIBLIOTHÈQUE NATIONALE 4106.
DANSE MACABRÉE DES FEMMES.
—PARISIIS, GUIDO MARCHANT, 1491,
2 MAII.

14 ffnc,; car. goth. 2 grand., type 2 (gros car. Thierry-Poux VIII, 2,
3 et Claudin I, pp. 336–337 au haut), type 6 (Pet. car. Claudin I, p.
397, alph. et p. 337 au bas); 35 ll.; signat. a, b, par 8 et 6 ff.; gravures;
init. grav. C (Claudin, I, p. 337); in-fol.

Bibliography

Ariès, Philippe. *L'Homme devant la mort*. Paris: Editions du Seuil, 1977.

————. *Western Attitudes toward Death: From the Middle Ages to the Present*. Baltimore: Johns Hopkins Univ. Press, 1974.

Boase, T. S. R. *Death in the Middle Ages: Mortality, Judgment and Remembrance*. London: Thames and Hudson, 1972.

Castelain, M.-F. *Au Pays de Claude de France*. [Romorantin:] Société d'Art, d'histoire et d'archéologie de Sologne, 1986.

Champion, Pierre, ed. *La Danse Macabre de Guy Marchant*. Paris: Editions des Quatre Chemins, 1925.

Chartier, R. "Les Arts de mourir (1450–1600)." *Annales: Economies, Sociétés, Civilisations* 31 (1976): 51–75.

Chaunu, Pierre. *La Mort à Paris: XVIe, XVIIe, XVIIIe siècles*. Paris: Fayard, 1978.

Chazaud, A.-M., ed. *Les Enseignements d'Anne de France duchesse de Bourbonnais et d'Auvergne à sa fille Susanne de Bourbon*. Moulins: C. Desrosiers, 1878.

Cotgrave, Randle. *A Dictionaire of the French and English Tongues*. Edited by William S. Woods. Columbia: Univ. of South Carolina Press, 1968.

Delisle, L. *Cabinet des Manuscrits de la Bibliothèque Imperiale Paris*, 3 vols. Paris, 1868.

Dubruck, Edelgard. "Another Look at 'macabre.'" *Romania* 79 (1958): 536–43.

————. *The Theme of Death in French Poetry of the Middle Ages and the Renaissance*. Brussels: Mouton, 1964.

Dufour, Antoine and G. Jeanneau. *Les Vies des femmes célèbres*. Geneva: Librairie Droz, 1970.

Dufour, V. *La Danse macabre des Saints Innocents de Paris d'après l'édition de 1484, précédée d'une étude sur le cimetiere, le charnier et la fresque peinte en 1425*. Paris: Léon Willem, 1874.

Durville, G. *Catalogue des manuscrits du Musée Dobrée*. Nantes: Musée Dobrée, 1904.

Götz, Louise. "Martial d'Auvergne: La Dance des Femmes." *Zeitschrift fur franzosische Sprache und Litteratur* 58 (1934): 318–34.

Grisay, A., G. Lavis, and M. Dubois-Stasse. *Les Dénominations de LA FEMME dans les anciens textes littéraires français*. Gembloux: 1969.

Hammerstein, Reinhold. *Tanz und Musik des Todes: Die mittelalter-lichen Totentanze und ihr Nachleben*. Bern: Francke Verlag, 1980.

Harrison, Ann Tukey. "Fifteenth-Century French Women's Role Names." *The French Review* 62 (1989): 436–44.

———. "La Grant Danse Macabre des Femmes." *Fifteenth-Century Studies* 3 (1980): 81–91.

Huizinga, J. *The Waning of the Middle Ages*. 1924. Reprint. New York: Doubleday, 1954.

Ivins, W. *The Dance of Death printed at Paris in 1490. A Reproduction made from the copy in the Lessing J. Rosenwald Collection*. Washington, D.C.: Library of Congress, 1945.

Kalbfleisch, Julia, ed. *Le Triumphe des Dames von Olivier de la Marche. Ausgabe nach den Handschriften. Inaugural Disserta-tion . . . Universitat Bern*. Rostock: H. Warkentien, 1901.

Kastner, J.-G. *Les Danses des morts, dissertations et recherches his-toriques, philosophiques, littéraires et musicales sur les divers mon-uments de ce genre . . .* Paris: Brandus, 1852.

Laffont, Robert, et al., eds. *The Illustrated History of Paris and the Parisians*. Translated by Isabel Quigly and Barbara Bray. New York: Doubleday, 1958.

Le Roux de Lincy. *Le Livre des proverbes français, I, II*. Paris: Paulin, 1842.

———. *La Vie d'Anne de Bretagne femme des rois de France*. 2 vols. Paris: L. Curmer, 1860–61.

Markale, Jean. *Anne de Bretagne*. Paris: Hachette, 1980.

Martial d'Auvergne. *Les Arrets d'Amour*. Edited by Jean Rychner. Paris: A. & J. Picard, 1951.

Meiss, Millard. "La Mort et l'Office des Morts à l'époque du Maître de Boucicaut et des Limbourgs." *Revue de l'Art* 1–2 (1968): 17–25.

Michelant, M. "Inventaire de la librairie de Marguerite d'Autriche, le 9 juillet, 1523." *Bulletin de la commission royale d'histoire de Bel-gique*, 3d series, 22 (1871): 5–78, 83–136.

Miot-Frochot, P.-L., ed. *La Grant Dance Macabre des Femmes que composa Maistre Marcial de Paris dit d'Auvergne procureur au parlement de Paris publie pour la première fois d'après le manuscrit unique de la Bibliothèque Imperiale*. Paris: Librairie Bachelin-Deflorenne, 1869.

Molitor, Ulric. *De Lamiis et Phitonicis Mulieribus*. Cologne: Cornelius von Zierikzee, 1489.

Monceaux, Henri. *Les Le Rouge de Chablis, calligraphes et miniatur-istes graveurs et imprimeurs, Etude sur les débuts de l'illustration du livre au XVe siècle*. Paris: A. Claudin, 1896.

Mortimer, Ruth, comp. *Catalogue of Books and Manuscripts*. 2 parts in 4 vols. Part 1, *French 16th Century Books*. 2 vols. Harvard College Library. Department of Printing and Graphic Arts. Cambridge: Belknap Press for Harvard Univ. Press, 1964–74.

O'Conner, Sister Mary Catharine. *The Art of Dying Well: The De-velopment of the Ars Moriendi*. New York: Columbia Univ. Press, 1942.

Orth, Myra Dickman. "Francis DuMoulin and Louise of Savoy." *The Sixteenth Century Journal* 13 (1982): 55–66.

Plummer, John, comp. *The Last Flowering: French Painting in Manu-scripts 1420–1530 from American Collections*. New York: Oxford Univ. Press, 1982.

Pradel, Pierre. *Anne de France 1461–1522*. Paris: Editions Publisud, 1986.

Praet, Joseph van. *Catalogue des livres imprimés sur vélin de la Bibliothèque du Roi*, 6 vols. Paris: Chez de Bure Frères, 1822–28.

Puttonen, Vilho. *Etudes sur Martial d'Auvergne*. Helsinki, 1943.

Rosenfeld, Helmut. *Der mittelalterliche Totentanz: Entstehung-Entwicklung-Bedeutung*. 2d ed. Cologne: Bohlau, 1968.

Rychner, Jean, ed. *Les Arrêts d'Amour de Martial d'Auvergne*. Paris: A. and J. Picard, 1951.

Sankovitch, Tilde. "Death and the Mole: Two Fifteenth-Century Dances of Death." *Fifteenth-Century Studies* 2 (1979): 211–17.

Saugnieux, J. *Les Danses macabres de France et d'Espagne et leurs prolongements littéraires*. Lyons: Emmanuel Vitte, 1972.

Soleil, F. *Les Heures gothiques et la littérature pieuse aux XVe et XVIe siècles*. Rouen: E. Augé, 1882.

Sterling, C. *The Master of Claude Queen of France, a Newly Defined Miniaturist*. New York: H. P. Kraus, 1975.

Tenenti, A. *Il sense della morte et l'amore della vita nel Rinascimento*. Turin: Giulio Einaudi Editore, 1957.

———. *La Vie et la mort à travers le XVe siècle. Cahiers des annales.* Series 8. Paris: Librairie Armand Colin, 1952.

Vaillant, Pierre. *La Danse macabre de 1485*. Grenoble: Editions des Quatre Seigneurs, 1969.

Wemple, Suzanne F. and Denise A. Kaiser. "Death's Dance of Women." *Journal of Medieval History* 12 (1986).

Winn, Mary Beth. "Books for a Princess and Her Son, Louise of Savoie, Françoise d'Angoulême and the Parisian Libraire Antoine Verard." *Bibliothèque d'Humanisme et Renaissance* 46 (1984): 603–17.

Zerner, H. "L'Art au Morier." *Revue de l'Art* 11 (1971): 7–30.

Index

The Danse Macabre *of Women*

was composed in Palatino text type
and Weiss display type
on a Penta system with CG8600 and L300 output
by Berman Electronic Prepress, Inc.;
printed by sheetfed offset on 70-pound acid-free
Crosspoint Torchglow Colonial White Opaque Smooth stock,
with color plates printed on 80-pound dull enamel stock,
Smyth sewn and case bound into 88′ binder's boards
in Holliston Kingston Natural cloth
with 80-pound Rainbow endpapers,
and wrapped with dustjackets printed in five colors
on 100-pound gloss enamel stock with film lamination
by BookCrafters, Inc.;
designed by Will Underwood;
and published by

The Kent State University Press
KENT, OHIO 44242